Abiding at the Feet of Jesus

A Study on the Beatitudes

Nate Sweeney

Sermon To Book
www.sermontobook.com

Abiding at the Feet of Jesus / Nate Sweeney
ISBN-13: 978-1-945793-52-3
ISBN-10: 1-945793-52-X

CONTENTS

Abiding in Christ

I am the true vine, and My Father is the vinedresser. Every branch in Me that does not bear fruit He takes away; and every branch that bears fruit He prunes, that it may bear more fruit.

You are already clean because of the word which I have spoken to you. Abide in Me, and I in you. As the branch cannot bear fruit of itself, unless it abides in the vine, neither can you, unless you abide in Me. I am the vine, you are the branches. He who abides in Me, and I in him, bears much fruit; for without Me you can do nothing.

If anyone does not abide in Me, he is cast out as a branch and is withered; and they gather them and throw them into the fire, and they are burned. If you abide in Me, and My words abide in you, you will ask what you desire, and it shall be done for you. By this My Father is glorified, that you bear much fruit; so you will be My disciples.

As the Father loved Me, I also have loved you; abide in My love. If you keep My commandments, you will abide in My love, just as I have kept My Father's commandments and abide in His love. These things I have spoken to you, that My joy may remain in you, and that your joy may be full.

This is My commandment, that you love one another as I have loved you. Greater love has no one than this, than to lay down one's life for his friends. You are My friends if you do whatever I command you. No longer do I call you servants, for a servant does not know what his master is doing; but I have called you friends, for all things that I heard from My Father I have made known to you.

You did not choose Me, but I chose you and appointed you that you should go and bear fruit, and that your fruit should remain, that whatever you ask the Father in My name He may give you. These things I command you, that you love one another.

—John 15:1–17

To abide means to continue to remain connected. What better place to remain connected to Christ than sitting at His feet and learning from Him as He articulates the foundations of His kingdom? John 15 paints a beautiful picture of a life that is connected to the vine of Christ. This life produces Kingdom fruit that remains in the realm of eternity.

Some key thoughts about John 15:1–17:

- Note the intimacy between Christ and the Father.

- Note the intimacy that Christ wants with us, just like He has with the Father.

- Note the seriousness with which He speaks about bearing fruit and the consequences for those who do not.

- Note the total dependence on Him that we must have.

- Note how our prayer life changes when we abide in Him and have His heart.

- Note how the Father is glorified when we bear Kingdom fruit.

- Note the importance of love in this passage, how walking in His love is connected to our obeying His commands and loving others.

The Beatitudes, found in Matthew 5, are a blueprint that you can follow on your journey into a rich and meaningful intimacy with Christ, that ultimately produces Kingdom fruit. Our study in the pages ahead focuses on some of the richest and most foundational words of Christ. These words, when applied, have the power to transform you and lead you into this intimate, abiding relationship. The goal of the Beatitudes is to pierce the heart of a religious, works-based, self-righteous culture and replace it with an intimate, abiding relationship with a living God.

The Beatitudes

And seeing the multitudes, [Jesus] went up on a mountain, and when He was seated His disciples came to Him. Then He opened His mouth and taught them, saying:

"Blessed are the poor in spirit, for theirs is the kingdom of heaven.

"Blessed are those who mourn, for they shall be comforted.

"Blessed are the meek, for they shall inherit the earth.

"Blessed are those who hunger and thirst for righteousness, for they shall be filled.

"Blessed are the merciful, for they shall obtain mercy.

"Blessed are the pure in heart, for they shall see God.

"Blessed are the peacemakers, for they shall be called sons of God.

"Blessed are those who are persecuted for righteousness' sake, for theirs is the kingdom of Heaven.

"Blessed are you when they revile and persecute you, and say all kinds of evil against you falsely for My sake. Rejoice and be exceedingly glad, for great is your reward in heaven, for so they persecuted the prophets who were before you."

—Matthew 5:1–12

The Latin word for "blessed" here is *beatus*, from which we get the word *beatitude*.[1] In fact, each statement of Christ's begins with, "Blessed are." This statement is then followed up with two more statements. The first one describes *who* is blessed, and the second one explains *how* they are blessed. So, these Beatitudes are giving us Kingdom insight into God's nature. If you want to be blessed, you must seek to be the kind of person He describes in these important verses.

What do these seemingly contradictory statements mean to us today? Many of these Beatitudes do not seem to make sense. In fact, many of the statements seem to be paradoxical. What did Jesus mean when He said that the poor in spirit are blessed and that the heavenly kingdom is theirs? How could someone be blessed in the midst of mourning? Was Jesus speaking in vague, abstract terms? What did He want us to take away from this sermon?

A writer once said this about the Beatitudes: It's like someone went into the display window of life and switched all the price tags, and what we thought had value suddenly didn't. We will find statements like, "happy are the sad," or "satisfied are the hungry." None of it makes sense until you place yourself at the feet of Jesus on a mountainside over two thousand years ago.[2]

Theology Versus Doctrine

All of us live our lives through our distinctive perspectives and mindsets. How we learn and understand scripture is affected by where we were raised, by our families, and through our unique life experiences. How you relate to God and to theology is tightly connected to your experiences in life. Most of you who are reading this have some hurts, habits, and hang-ups in life, and these cause you to struggle with God. So, your perspective is based on what you have experienced.

In order to lay a foundation that allows you to read the pages ahead with a cleared perspective, we need to understand from the beginning that biblical doctrine is authoritative. That authority is clearly defined in the Bible, and if you are a follower of Christ, there is no bending or twisting doctrine. It is what it is, being from God, and man gets no say-so in it. We don't bend doctrine. Doctrine does not change based on your circumstances, nor does it necessarily align with your experiences.

Theology, on the other hand, is different from doctrine. In essence, *theology* means the study of God. All of us view God differently based on our experiences. Your journey is very different from anyone else's, and your understanding of God has taken a path different from anyone else's. This does not change God or the doctrine of the Bible. It only speaks to how you learned about and understand God and the doctrine that He has prescribed to us. The reason this is so important is, if you are not careful, you will read the words of Christ and view them through the lenses of your own theology, and then you may miss some vitally transformational pieces for your life.

Years ago, a lady at a church I pastored was offended that we celebrated Mother's Day as a church. She was an orphan and she had a lot of pain associated even with the mention of mothers. In talking with her, my heart broke. Through a long season of prayer, biblical counseling, and loving people pouring into her life, we were able to help her see all the spiritual mothers that God had placed in her life. She found healing and joy, and she eventually used her story to minister to people with similar histories. God used the very thing that once caused her such pain and agony to make her a catalyst in others' lives for healing and freedom.

Because of her pain, this woman struggled to celebrate Mother's Day. However, that didn't mean that the day shouldn't be celebrated or that it was right for her to be angry at all mothers. At the beginning, she wanted her theology of Mother's Day to be doctrine for our church.

You may be reading this and be tempted to give up and put this book down. You might feel that you have too much sin in your life or too much baggage to draw near to Jesus. You may think there is too much pain, and you cannot see the other side of healing. Take those goggles off.

Put off all of that junk from your past—your sorrow and your pain—and give Christ an opportunity to love you.

In the pages ahead, we are going to explore how God's kingdom in heaven is wide open for you today. God can help you find healing from your painful past experiences and help you discover new, joyous ones in Him. He wants to change your perspective. He wants to challenge your theology. He wants to remove religious things, and He invites you to abide with Him.

The Swoosh

Years ago, in prayer, I had a vision of a day when I would author many books that would help spread the gospel of Christ to the nations. During that vision, I saw what I could only describe as a smeared fingerprint. I knew what it meant immediately. In the environment I grew up around, we took the biblical model of anointing with oil seriously. If you have ever taken some oil on your finger and applied it to a doorpost, to someone's forehead, or to a sheet of paper, you know the smeared fingerprint that is left behind. In this vision, I had the understanding that I wanted to anoint each copy of the books, which would leave that smeared look. I wrote this in my journal and left it there.

Years later, as I began to see the dreams of authoring Christ-centered books come to pass, I was reminded of this. Although I cannot personally anoint every book, I decided to use what I call a swoosh to designate that each book has been prayed over. My prayer is that the words in the books published will be anointed by God, bring life transformation to all who read them, and bring glory to God.

Workbook Sections with a Journal Prompt

At the end of each chapter in this book, you will find application-focused workbook sections that will help you delve deeper into the material and develop concrete steps to put the abiding principles to work for your individual and congregational needs. In each workbook section, there will be a journal prompt. In Appendix A, you will find the STAR journaling grid, which is designed to help you discover how to journal in a meaningful way.[3]

We want you to understand that journaling is another form of communication with God and can become a lifestyle. This can happen if you feel connected to God through His Word. This connection happens when you read His Word and apply it to your life in the circumstances you are dealing with.

As we move forward in this book, it is important that you understand that the process you will be going through will require that you learn to "self-feed" in God's Word. You can get a journal to accommodate this book or use whatever works best for you. In using the journal, you will experience a process that will help you become a self-feeder. This process will likely continue for the rest of your life. I understand that most people initially feel a little intimidated with journaling until they come to see that it is not as hard or as complicated as they feared it would be.

About The Abiding Network

The vision of The Abiding Network, of which I am the founder and directional leader, is to assist leaders in creating environments of discipleship to encourage followers to know Christ and make Him known.

Abiding Network was launched out of Catalyst Church in Bentonville, Arkansas, in 2013. This is a support network for church leaders who are active in ministry to know Christ and make Him known in their area of influence.

Our heart is to network individuals, churches, nonprofits, and other groups to support their Kingdom calling. We offer a system of biblical accountability, encouragement, relationship building, and resource sharing to assist in their health and long-term success.

As a network, we have partnered with dozens of churches in many diverse areas. Our website (http://www.abidingnetwork.com) offers some of the organizations and ministries with which we have partnered for Kingdom fruit. As our network grows, we add ministries to our platform so that the network expands as God leads.

The intent of Abiding Network members should be to unite in the common vision to know Christ and make Him known. We want a unity of the Spirit that celebrates what God is doing in our world today.

Coaching

Many leaders in the business and church worlds need

an outside voice for encouragement, accountability, leadership development, and organizational strategy. One aspect of The Abiding Network is to serve leaders in such a capacity—for instance, in seasons of building, transition, growth, relationship development, tragedy, and celebration. Some of the most fruitful seasons of our lives can be birthed out of a mentor or coach helping us process through our journey.

We also are developing many leadership resources that are available to help church leaders navigate the short- and long-term direction and vision of their sphere of influence. I personally have been coached, and I myself coach many leaders in many different ministry and secular environments. I have found coaching to be one of the greatest catalysts to my personal and professional growth and leadership development. Sometimes we simply need a coach, like Paul was to Timothy, to help us grow into all that God intends for us.

Resources

For more information about The Abiding Network, please visit www.abidingnetwork.com. Media resources can be found at http://www.abidingnetwork.com/Media.

And please see Appendix B of this book for information about the Journey program and the Influencers ministry, as well as a list of relevant resources—including my books *The Abiding Church* and *Abiding in Identity*, also published by Sermon To Book.

I appreciate you taking the time to check out these resources in addition to reading this book. Thank you for your interest in The Abiding Network.

And may this book help you grow into a deeper understanding of what it means to abide at the feet of Jesus.

—*Nate Sweeney*

.

CHAPTER ONE

Setting the Scene

Have you ever been in a situation where, no matter what you do or how much you try, you just can't get ahead? Perhaps you went to college, earned your degree, but can't find a job in your field of study, so you end up taking an entry-level job and are living paycheck to paycheck just to get by. All the while, your student loans continue to accrue interest because you can only afford to pay the minimum payment.

Maybe you're attempting to save for a trip or a home, but every time you turn around another unplanned expense crops up, emptying your savings account yet again.

I imagine the people who sat at Jesus' feet in Matthew 5 felt a lot like this.

At the time that Jesus gave His Sermon the Mount, the Jews in the Promised Land were under the rule of the Roman government. Like most of the people groups conquered by the Romans, the Jews struggled to pay the heavy taxes and to obey the often-unfair laws under the watch of the Roman army. The Jews prayed for freedom from the Roman government and believed that the promised Messiah would rise up and conquer their oppressors.

The Sanhedrin was a group of Jewish men who were the ultimate authority for all Jews. However, the Romans demanded that they submit to Roman laws. The few Jews who gained power as tax collectors were often dishonest, taking bribes, overcharging their fellow Jews, and keeping the additional money for themselves.[4]

Life in the time of Christ was often unfair. Men were considered far superior to women, who had few rights. The Roman government and military oppressed all their conquered peoples. Jews considered themselves far superior to all other races. Roman religions preached the worship of many gods, which promoted indulging in sexual exploration, debauchery, and excessive feasting.

Even among the Jews, there was a variety of beliefs about God. Synagogues were built so that people could worship when they couldn't get to the temple in Jerusalem. The rabbi placed at the synagogue was a scholar of the Old Testament who taught the local boys. Rigidly keeping the Law became more important than knowing God. There was a move toward legalism—technically following rules while skirting the full intent of them.

New laws were added that weren't told to the prophets by God. The various groups of Jews disagreed on how certain laws should be observed. Some thought that these new man-made rules were to be followed as strictly as the Old Testament laws. The Pharisees, Sadducees, zealots, and Essenes all claimed to be doing what was right but claimed that everyone else was wrong.

Being born into a family of Pharisees or Sadducees meant a life of studying the Old Testament, which often produced a sense of spiritual superiority. Members of these sects looked down on the average Jew, believing that they weren't as learned and were less deserving of God's blessings than sect members were.[5]

The end result was an entire group of lost, broken individuals who had little hope of their lives ever being full of the riches that God had promised His people. Jesus came to change all of that.

The Setting of the Beatitudes

Jesus' ministry began once He returned from being tempted in the desert (Matthew 4:1–12). He came back ready to begin teaching about God's Word, healing the sick, and ministering to the multitudes. It would have made sense for Him to kick everything off in a big way, but that wasn't how things happened.

Instead, Jesus withdrew from the crowd and went to a mountainside to quietly teach disciples. Despite His attempts to be alone, the crowds found them, and what resulted was what some people say is the best sermon ever. This sermon, usually called the "Sermon on the Mount," is found in Matthew 5, 6, and 7. It starts with Jesus describing the Beatitudes.

The Essence of Each Beatitude

As you read this book, notice that the beginning of each chapter will define the essence of the Beatitude in that chapter. Jesus was an amazing teacher, and He did not disappoint in these Beatitudes. Each Beatitude carries a very specific meaning and a significant individual feature. However, the Beatitudes seem to be systematic and progressive. This means that you cannot effectively jump ahead to the next Beatitude without embracing and digesting the previous one. The fruit of each Beatitude opens revelation to the next one. This is important to note so that you don't gloss over any aspect of the message.

And so, we will begin with the poor in spirit.

WORKBOOK

Chapter One Questions

Question: What is the cultural context for the Beatitudes? Describe life for the average follower of Jesus at the time of His ministry on earth?

_____

_____

_____

_____

_____

_____

_____

_____

_____

_____

_____

Question: Describe the beginning of Jesus' public ministry. Why do you think He chose such an unassuming start?

_____

_____

_____

_____

_____

_____

_____

_____

_____

_____

_____

Question: Why is it important to study the Beatitudes in order that Jesus taught them?

_____

_____

_____

_____

_____

_____

_____

_____

_____

_____

_____

_____

Action: Read Appendix A to learn about the STAR journaling process. Plan to journal using the prompts at the end of each chapter.

Journal: For your first STAR journal entry, read and meditate on Matthew 4 to understand the immediate context for the Sermon on the Mount-oriented summary.

Chapter One Notes

CHAPTER TWO

The Poor in Spirit

Blessed are the poor in spirit, for theirs is the kingdom of heaven.

—Matthew 5:3

Who are the "poor" of whom Jesus speaks in His message here? Is it the woman on the street holding a sign asking for help purchasing food for her young children? Is it the refugee who has been driven from his country, losing everything in the process, only to come to a land where he feels just as unwelcome as he was in the land of his birth?

When Jesus used the phrase "poor in spirit," was He trying to say that the economically poor are actually blessed? I know that many people have interpreted this verse in that way. When looking at Luke's record of Christ's message, He doesn't use the words "in spirit." He simply says, "Blessed are you poor."

On other occasions, Christ talks about how hard it is

for a rich man to enter the Kingdom. So, it begs the question: Is God anti-riches and pro-poverty?

That is not the overarching idea that the Bible gives us about money. As we study scripture, we discover that it is not the riches themselves that make it hard for a person to get to heaven. It is the attitude that we don't need help that is the problem. A person who is poor knows that he needs help and he is often more comfortable asking for it than someone who is accustomed to being self-sufficient.

It's important to note that Matthew 5:3 clearly refers to a poor spirit, not to finances. Whether or not you have money does not automatically reflect the state of your spiritual life. The Greek word for "poor" in this case is *ptochos* (toe-KAS). This word has a very specific meaning: one who is reduced to begging dependence; someone who is bankrupt.[6]

In other words, *the essence of "poor in spirit" means that the Kingdom of Christ is for the repentant, spiritually bankrupt, dependent, and needy person. Material wealth has no bearing on this matter.*

Spiritual Brokenness

I don't know about you, but the idea of having a church full of broken people doesn't sound terribly appealing. How would I bring my friends? I'd be so embarrassed. Yet Jesus says that people who are spiritually broken are blessed! It's the people who are aware of the depths of their sin who receive this blessing, not the ones who have it all together. How countercultural!

Christ wants us to know that His kingdom is for the

beggar, the bankrupt, and the broken. The theological backdrop of the gospel is the total depravity of humanity. The Kingdom of God is not for the religious people who know how to say and do the "right" things, nor is it for the self-righteous. God is looking for people who know that, in and of themselves, they cannot do it all right. They are reduced to a beggarly dependence on God to work in and through them. They need help, and they understand that.

If people do not understand their need for the Savior, they will never move toward repentance. And if we do not repent, the gospel can have no effect in our lives. This understanding of our need for Christ is the beautiful message that Jesus wrapped up by His simple statement, "Blessed are the poor in spirit, for theirs is the kingdom of God."

God is a loving Father who, through our repentance, will forgive us our sins and cleanse us. Equally, however, He is a just, wrathful judge who condemns those who've rejected Him, trusting in their own righteousness to save them. The catalyst for redemption is repentance (Acts 2:38–39).

It's impossible for us to abide with Christ if we refuse to see ourselves as sinful. That attitude will always keep God at arm's length. It denies what was done for us on the cross and calls God a liar.

If you reflect on your sin and find yourself thinking, "I'm not too bad, I don't sin very much," you need to ask God to show you the truth about yourself. The Holy Spirit is always ready to begin to reveal what's really happening in your heart. As you acknowledge your sin issues, confess them to God and ask for forgiveness. Confession and repentance draw us to God faster than anything else.

There are many mindsets contrary to the gospel that crept into the Church many years ago that are now making a resurgence. One of these false philosophies is the mindset that man is inherently good. This is taught in many circles outside of the Christian world, but in recent days it, is turning up in the Church more and more. This mindset declares divinity to be in all humanity and says that we simply need enlightenment to discover that goodness and live it out. This is exactly opposite to the gospel message and the message of spiritual poverty, which we are studying here. Many professed Christians are being deceived and drawn away into false gospels. We need this foundation of the Beatitudes in order to live a transformed walk with Christ.

The Difference Between the Pharisee and the Tax Collector

Also [Jesus] spoke this parable to some who trusted in themselves that they were righteous, and despised others: "Two men went up to the temple to pray, one a Pharisee and the other a tax collector. The Pharisee stood and prayed thus with himself, 'God, I thank You that I am not like other men—extortioners, unjust, adulterers, or even as this tax collector. I fast twice a week; I give tithes of all that I possess.' And the tax collector, standing afar off, would not so much as raise his eyes to heaven, but beat his breast, saying, 'God, be merciful to me a sinner!' I tell you, this man went down to his house justified rather than the other; for everyone who exalts himself will be humbled, and he who humbles himself will be exalted."

—Luke 18:9–14

The Pharisee was quick to condemn all the "evildoers," especially the tax collector standing outside. He also had a list of all the behaviors that affirmed his righteousness, things he believed would make him right with God. He had to feel pretty good about himself. His idea of spirituality was wrapped up in both what he didn't do (thievery, adultery, etc.) and what he did do (attend services, tithe, and fast). He fell in line with everyone else's expectations. Matters of the heart were not important. This man did not understand his need for a savior. He was not broken or dependent on anyone. In the words of Jesus, he walked away condemned and not justified.

It said the tax collector stood "afar off." It seems as if his own condemnation would not even let him go inside the temple to pray. He didn't feel like he was good enough to go to church, believing that church was a place for good people who no longer struggled with sin. He understood that he had nothing to offer and that he wholly needed God in his life. He recognized that he was a sinner and needed a savior. This is the place where God wants all of us to be.

According to Christ, this man walked away justified— not because of his self-loathing, but because he recognized that in and of himself he was depraved and needed God. He cried out to God in repentance and need. Therefore, God justified this man and not the other.

Who would you rather be in this parable? We all know the right answer that Christ gave, but deep down most of us struggle with wanting to be the guy who had it all together. We try to be the one who looks good and who doesn't have any problems.

I've spent a lot of energy in life on having it together

and being independent and trying to have all the right answers.

What about you? The tax agent went home justified by God, not the Pharisee. He reached a point of brokenness and beggarly dependence on God. He said things that equated to, "I can't," "I need help," "You are my only hope," "I try," "I fail," and "I need You."

Consolation and Confrontation

In every one of the Beatitudes, there is either a great consolation or a great confrontation, depending on which side you stand.

Consolation

"Blessed are the poor in spirit" was a great consolation to the tax agent, who was at the end of trying hard to do it right—knowing he never could. It was the same consolation given to Peter, who denied Christ after saying, "I will never leave you, I will follow you to death" (Matthew 26:35). It is always a consolation to people who reach the end of their strength. It is a consolation to you if you can reveal the real you that God knows and still loves.

If you can come to a place of understanding that you are sinful and cannot do anything to truly fix yourself, then you will find the promise of hope God gave us in Jesus. You will begin to say things like, "God, I tried, I failed, I am fully dependent on You. I need You in my life to help and guide me. I am bankrupt without You and wholly dependent on You, God." His loving grace comes and frees you from the self-righteousness, condemnation, and sin under which you have been living. This is a great consolation and freedom to those who find it.

Confrontation

As with all truths, the "poor in spirit" message will confront you and cause you to come to a place of decision. When God begins to reveal His Word to you, you have the option to obey or disobey. Obedience brings the blessing, and disobedience brings the consequences. We see in the lives of Peter, Paul, and the early disciples that their poverty in spirit translated into great power, numerous confrontations with the powers of darkness, and amazing activity for the Kingdom of Christ. When they chose to obey the Word of God and live in a daily posture of dependence, God was able to move in their lives and confirm His Word to them.

Many times, the Word of God is offensive to us because it confronts our sin and weakness, and we don't like that. When we refuse to acknowledge our sin, we are setting ourselves in opposition to the way God designed us to live.

When people try to find their own way to salvation, they experience fruits of selfishness, pride, and ego. This is not beggarly dependence and will cause us to miss out on the blessings of being "poor in spirit." If Jesus says that those are the ones who will inherit the kingdom of heaven, what will happen for those who are *not* willing to examine their brokenness and bring their repentance before the Father?

The sad thing is that many times we prefer to be like the Pharisee rather than the tax collector in that parable. We don't want to see what we're doing wrong. We don't want to recognize our sin, because then we'll have to do something about it. We'd rather go on doing what we know we shouldn't do because it's comfortable, because it feeds our sinful nature, or because it would take too much work to change.

On the other hand, what happens if we address our sin through this posture of poor in spirit and cry out for forgiveness and healing, like the tax collector did in Luke 18? We would find comfort, forgiveness, restoration, and the Kingdom of God. This is a great consolation that is available to you right now. The foundation of biblical brokenness (*ptochos* [TOE-kas]) opens the door to walk through the other Beatitudes.

WORKBOOK

Chapter Two Questions

Question: What does being "poor in spirit" mean? How is it related and/or not related to financial poverty?

_____

_____

_____

_____

_____

_____

_____

_____

_____

_____

_____

_____

Question: With whom do you identify the most in the parable of the Pharisee and the tax collector? Which one would those who know you well say that you are the most like?

_____

_____

_____

_____

_____

_____

_____

_____

_____

_____

_____

Action: The Pharisee gave a list of all his good deeds in comparison to the "really bad" sins of others. What legalistic standards or legitimate good works cause you to be proud and self-righteous? What types of people do you tend to see as inferior to yourself?

Journal: Meditate on Matthew 5:3. Ask the Holy Spirit to reveal your sin to you and to show you where your heart is hard, self-righteous, or self-sufficient. How will you walk in dependence on God?

Chapter Two Notes

_____

_____

_____

_____

_____

_____

_____

_____

_____

_____

_____

_____

_____

_____

_____

_____

_____

_____

_____

_____

_____

_____

_____

_____

_____

CHAPTER THREE

Those Who Mourn

Blessed are those who mourn, for they shall be comforted.
—Matthew 5:4

Have you ever heard someone say, "I had a good cry and got it all out. I feel much better now" after experiencing some sort of emotional or physical grief?

Most people feel better after letting out their hurt and frustrations through a healthy emotional release. The ability to move what is inside to the outside is absolutely essential for our emotional health, whether we understand it or not.

God designed us this way. It's like He gave us an emotional pressure valve that allows us to release the feelings we have deep down. When we choose to get them out, we find comfort. When we continue to press them down, it can result in depression, physical pain, or complete isolation.

Some of the most unhappy, hard-to-be-around people

are the ones who have never given themselves permission to get outside what is going on in the inside. They are frustrated and bottled up. In other words, they fail to mourn.

The essence of biblical mourning is an act of reflection, cleansing, healing, and expression. It allows us to reflect the image of God out of a pure and redeemed heart.

Remember the setting where Jesus was preaching this message. The Jews who were listening felt inferior to the religious leaders, who seemed to have it all together. Many of those who were hearing this message wanted to jump in with both feet, but their shameful self-image would not allow them to take the next step—that is, until Jesus expounded some more.

This Beatitude sounds a little like, "Happy are the sad." It is something that, if taken at face value, doesn't seem to make sense. What could possibly be blessed about mourning? Knowing that Jesus is Truth (John 14:6), we understand there must be more to this Beatitude. What did Jesus mean when He talked about mourning? Why did He describe this person as blessed? Let's take a closer look at what is being said here.

Here the word "mourning," in the original language, is *penthos*. *Penthos* (PEN-thos) is defined as an "external expression of an internal reality; an inner sorrow or condition that is outwardly demonstrated."[7]

There are different verbs for the word *mourn* in Greek, and this one is quite specific. It means an external expression of an internal reality. It is an inner sorrow or condition that is outwardly demonstrated.

Think of what happens when someone cries. As the

tears flow, people can see on the outside what is happening on the inside. Whether they are tears of sorrow or gladness, their outside expression shows that something is happening on the inside of that person.

Note the difference between this kind of mourning and the kind that you can hide from the world. Mourning an acquaintance is different from mourning someone you know well. The loss of an acquaintance will never affect your life in the enormous way that losing a close family member or a dear friend will.

In the Jewish culture, mourning was expressed in a lot of different ways. When certain tragedies occurred, people would weep loudly, shave or cover their heads, tear their clothes, wrap themselves with sackcloth, and put ashes on their foreheads (Job 2:12). All of this was an outward display of an inward sorrow.

When you experience *ptochos* (brokenness), you step over the threshold into *penthos* (mourning). Think about what you have to understand about your sin before you show outward signs of mourning. What would have to be happening in your heart for you to make outward changes to stop sinning?

Keeping It Real

Jim and Carol looked like they had it all together. Their home was beautifully decorated with interesting artifacts they gathered on their world travels. Both of them regularly posted pictures of the gourmet meals they ate, the professional sports events they had season tickets to attend, and cruises they participated in during their vacations. They had two adorable children who were always well dressed and smiling whenever the camera was out.

But the reality of Jim and Carol's life together was very different on the inside. Jim's temper meant that he was often verbally abusive and occasionally physically abusive to his family. Carol's excessive spending meant that they were drowning in debt and considering filing for bankruptcy. Their children were stuck in daycare because their parents both had to work very long hours to pay for their extravagant lifestyle.

If you met Jim or Carol on the street and asked them how they were doing, they'd point to all the "good" things they had going on, without once acknowledging the trouble brewing beneath the surface. Not necessarily because they were embarrassed, but because of their pride.

In Galatians 6:13 Paul speaks of people who boast in the flesh. These are people who believe that the way things look on the outside is what really matters and that everything is okay as long as we look good to the world. Ultimately, it becomes more important for them to make others think they have it all together. But when we live our lives in this manner—when we bottle everything up, refusing to acknowledge our hurts, struggles, or sin—the cost can be steep.

Some of us have been given a message that good Christians don't sin and/or they don't get hurt. They don't stumble or get scared. Emotion is weakness and unnecessary. If they do feel emotionally broken, they don't show it, because they have been told it is more "spiritual" to hide it.

These beliefs are far from true. If you don't learn to biblically mourn, eventually your pressure valve will get frozen with bitterness and offense. Your life will be headed for an emotional breakdown because of your inability to mourn.

The irony is that some of the saddest people in the world are those who never mourn. The truth is that good Christians do get hurt, they do struggle, they do get scared, and sometimes they fall flat on their faces in sin. The beauty of this Beatitude is that we can be blessed if we learn to move our pain outward and release it to God.

Consider the words of King David: "When I kept silent, my bones grew old, through my groaning all the day long. For day and night Your hand was heavy upon me; my vitality was turned into the drought of summer. Selah. I acknowledged my sin to You, and my iniquity I have not hidden. I said, 'I will confess my transgressions to the Lord,' And You forgave the iniquity of my sin" (Psalm 32:3–5).

What would it take for Jim and Carol to get the help they need? They would have to confess the depths of their problems, which would open them up to criticism. They would need to stop spending money, cut way back on their expenses, and pay off their debt. The image they presented to the world would take a serious hit.

And, unfortunately, in many churches, the pair's admittance of their problems could open them up to gossip. Too many congregations in America today are more concerned with going through the motions and having their appearances in place than with finding freedom from the sin problems that are pulling them down. When we worship other people's good opinions, we aren't able to worship Jesus as well.

The Spiritual Reality

When we enter into an attitude of spiritual poverty, our natural reaction is to mourn. This mourning can look different from person to person. Some of us turn to God and pour out our hearts to Him in thankful prayer. Some people make significant changes to their habits. For others, worship or acts of service are the way that they outwardly show that they understand their sin and what Jesus' salvation means to them.

I love the story from Luke chapter 7 about the prostitute and how she mourned her sin (Luke 7:36–50). Throughout the New Testament, we see Jesus interacting with people whom the religious men of His day would have avoided at all costs. In this story, Jesus was at dinner when a prostitute came into the room.

She stood behind Jesus, not saying a word, and began to weep. She knelt down and wiped His feet clean with her hair. Then she opened a bottle of alabaster and poured it on His feet. This woman understood the depths of her sin and the promise of redemption that Jesus offered.

The Pharisees were horrified by her inappropriate behavior. Jesus explained something to them that even their self-righteous and self-satisfying minds could understand: Those who have been forgiven much will love to that degree, and those who have been forgiven little will love to the same degree (Luke 7:47).

The reason for this woman's change of heart was her willingness to come face-to-face with her sin. She took responsibility for her sin and asked for redemption. The difference between the prostitute and the Pharisee was not that she was a sinner and he was righteous. They were both sinners. The difference was that she knew she was a sinner. She mourned her sin and found comfort. This is the way of Christ.

The Results of Release

The first result of revealing what is going on inside of us is comfort. The burden of hiding and pretending is automatically released. Jesus said the mourners would be comforted. That is His promise to us.

The second result is grace. The apostle John writes, "If we confess our sins He is faithful and just, and will forgive us our sins and purify us from all unrighteousness" (1 John 1:9). In the moment we tell God the whole truth about the wickedness in our hearts, we open the floodgates to forgiveness. Those who receive this amazing grace develop grateful hearts. They are motivated toward holiness because they have been empowered by unending mercy. This is what grace really does. We receive grace when we realize how much we need it and when we are willing to mourn our sin and get it out. Grief is meant to draw out of us the mercy and grace of God and provoke us to give that away to others.

Third, we get joy. As we deal with our sin, pain, and despair, the comfort and grace we receive sets us up for joy. You are truly blessed if you learn to release your sin, repent and turn away from it, and receive Christ's grace.

Hindrances to True Mourning

Because we live in a society that places value on independence and self-reliance, it can be difficult for us to recognize our need for help. The very traits the world celebrates as strengths are the ones that scripture continually warns us to watch out for. Let's take a look at just a few of these hindrances.

1. Pride

Jesus described people blinded by self-righteousness in Matthew 23:25. It reads, "Woe to you … you hypocrites! You clean the outside of the cup and dish, but the inside is full of greed and self-indulgence" (NIV). When we invest our whole lives in cultivating an image of righteousness, we are only concerned with what other people perceive. Mourning is viewed as weakness and as unacceptable. When we are so proud of our outward appearances of righteousness, we smugly look down on those who don't have it all together.

That's when things go wrong and we fall apart, all our superiority smacks us in the face, because we have to come to terms with our inability to control our lives. Facing the fullness of our inability to do what's right, when everything's falling apart, is devastating.

2. Fear of Disclosure

We can be so afraid of what people will think that we spend our entire lives hiding our pain and sorrow. It is easier to just maintain a good outward image rather than alter other people's good opinions of us.

God desires you to be free in Him and to experience His goodness. The process of healing and deliverance can be brutal, but it does not compare to the joy of freedom. Fear of man will keep you from fully abiding with Christ.

Some people have tried opening themselves up in the past, but they were rejected or shut down. Instead of comfort and grace, they discovered that people were horrified by what they said and even condemned them for saying it. This type of experience will cause a real hindrance to God's kind of mourning in the future. If you don't have a safe place to share about your sin issues, then please find one. A love-centered biblical community will encourage biblical mourning, knowing the Kingdom fruits it produces. You might need to seek out a spiritual friend who can help hold you accountable as you seek to change your life.

3. Inability to Manage Mourning

People with this fear feel that if they ever allow the mourning to begin, it just won't stop coming. There is so much pain and sorrow that they think that if one thing comes out, it will all spill out. This is a risk worth taking. Many times, I have seen people who think the pain of holding it all in is less than the pain and energy it takes to get it all out. They are deceived into thinking they are better off just holding on to their offense and hurt.

I have yet to meet a person who finally allowed God to take him or her through this process of mourning and came through it worse off than they started. Again, mourning opens the floodgates of God's comfort, grace, and joy. This can be a long, intensive process, but it is worth it in the end.

4. Self-Condemnation

Some of us feel that we are past forgiveness. We think we have gone so far that we are beyond the reach of Christ's grace. When we feel this way, we do not need others' judgment, because we are own worst critics. We live in the guilt of our own accusations, and we struggle to believe that God will forgive us. What if He knew all the bad things we have done? The truth is that God already knows all of those things and yet He is still aggressively pursuing you with His love and grace! None of us is so far gone that God's grace cannot save us.

5. Love of Our Sin

We have such a sneaky enemy, don't we? It's easy for us to look at a big sin and condemn it while secretly loving our own little sin. We know that gossiping is wrong, but it's just so satisfying to pass on a juicy comment about someone who has been bugging us. It's easy to point a finger at someone who sins differently than we do. This can blind us to our own sin.

The problem is that sin often feels good. Our sinful nature convinces us that it's not such a big deal, or that it's just a normal thing everyone does. How can we convince ourselves not to sin when we like it so much?

Begin by going to God. He already knows your sin better than you do, so go ahead and talk about it with Him. Confess what you're doing, what you're not doing, and the fact that you don't want to give it up. You can even confess that you don't feel like you have any sin. Ask God for freedom and to help you see your sin more clearly.

As we release to the outside what is going on inside, we will receive comfort, grace, and joy from God. It is vitally important to be completely open and honest so that we can confess sin and experience true godly sorrow.

When we become mourners, we begin to recognize people around us who are mourning their sin and we can extend them a hand of comfort and grace. We can become a safe place for them to confess and repent. You will live out Romans 12:15, which tells us to "rejoice with those who rejoice and mourn with those who mourn" (NIV).

Chapter Three Questions

Question: What is the specific kind of mourning that Jesus is addressing in this Beatitude?

_____

_____

_____

_____

_____

_____

_____

_____

_____

_____

Question: Describe some of the cultural differences between first-century mourning and mourning today. Compare and contrast mourning over sin and mourning over the loss of a loved one.

_____

_____

_____

_____

_____

_____

_____

_____

_____

_____

Action: Which of these is the greatest hindrance to you personally: pride, fear of disclosure, inability to manage mourning, self-condemnation, or love of your sin? How has this particular hindrance kept you from mourning your sin and receiving God's comfort? Seek out a mature Christian mentor or friend and ask them to keep you accountable to deal with this hindrance in your life.

Journal: Meditate on Matthew 5:4 and 1 John 1:9. Take time to reflect on both your sin and Christ's cleansing and healing.

Chapter Three Notes

CHAPTER FOUR

The Meek

Blessed are the meek, for they shall inherit the earth.
—***Matthew 5:5***

When Jesus showed up on the scene, most in Israel were waiting on the Messiah. He had been talked about and prophesied for many generations. The Jews of Jesus' day were hoping for a warrior who would throw off Roman rule and take control, reestablishing David's kingdom. After years of oppression, they were ready to be the top dogs in the empire. Instead they discovered a man who had the ability to control wind and waves, who could heal the blind and restore life to the dead, but who allowed Himself to be betrayed by one close to Him and ultimately be put to death in the most horrific manner known to mankind.

The world would have us believe that anyone who would allow others to control their lives are weak, and therefore to be despised. But Christ's example shows us the perfect picture of meekness. True meekness is anything but weakness.

The essence of a biblically meek individual is someone who understands the God-given power that ptochos *and* penthos *produce and who then submits to the authority of the Master. This produces gentleness and peace, which brings life to those around the individual.*

The synagogues were filled with Pharisees, chief priests, and scribes. In this system, the Kingdom of God was set aside for the religious elite, not for the broken, hungry, and mourning. In order to matter, you had to know the right terminology, wear the right clothing, have the right background—the list went on and on.

Jesus didn't ride in on a stallion, leading an army. He didn't spend all His time with the "holy" people. Instead, He ate meals with tax collectors, prostitutes, and other "sinners."

Imagine what would happen if Jesus came in our current times. Some would expect Him to hang out in the best churches, and to tell all of us what wonderful Christians we were. But I imagine that He would visit prisons, sit with the homeless, and eat meals with drug addicts and prostitutes. He would spend His time investing in those who understood their need for Him, and He would invite them into His kingdom.

"Blessed are the meek" sounds an awful lot like "Blessed are the weak" to me. When I hear this phrase, I often picture a timid and wimpy person who allows himself to be bullied because he's too afraid to stand up for himself.

What about you? If you overheard a conversation about

you in which you were called "meek," how would that make you feel? If you view the idea of meekness like most people do, chances are you would want to challenge that characterization of yourself.

The dictionary defines *meek* as "enduring injury with patience and without resentment; deficient in spirit and courage; not violent or strong."[8] That just reaffirms my perception that meek equals weak. So, what was Jesus really saying here? Was He affirming that weakness is honorable in His kingdom?

The Greek word for "meek" in this instance is *praÿs*. Its root means gentle, mild, or tender.[9] At first glance, that seems to affirm some of my beliefs about meekness. But as we explore its uses, especially in classical Greek, we get a better understanding of what Jesus was talking about.

Gentle and Soothing

Praÿs was used to describe a soothing medicine and a gentle breeze. In other words, blessed are those who are "a soothing medicine and a gentle breeze." I love that, especially when I am hurting and need someone to pick me up and encourage me. Those are the kind of people I want to run to when I don't have all the answers.

Have you ever met anyone who is a "gentle breeze" or a "soothing medicine"? When you talk to them, they have a calming effect on you. We all need to be connected to people who are a gentle breeze and a soothing medicine. When we stumble, fall, fail, hurt, and can't seem to come up with the right answers, it is these "meek" people who come to our side.

Unfortunately, we have all experienced people who are the exact opposite. When we begin to mourn, struggle, or go through a tough time, we run into people who are like rough sandpaper. In fact, if we're honest, I think we know that most of us have been these people to others at times ourselves.

Power Under Control

As we look deeper into the uses of this word, it broadens a bit further. *Praÿs* was also used in reference to taming wild animals.

Picture a wild horse that has been captured for the first time. It has spent its entire life totally free to do whatever it wanted to do, at any time. At first, it is uncontrollable and frightened of its captors. Its power and energy are endless, but it has no direction. It is dangerous and presently useless.

However, things change dramatically when the trainer is given the reins. Through a series of sometimes-painful lessons, the horse is "gentled" and is eventually able to be put to good work.

This is exactly the meaning of *praÿs*. Something once wild has been tamed. I like to think of it as power under control. It has direction and can serve a good purpose. It has become teachable and usable under the control of the Master.

Please note that a horse is not a weak animal. It does not lack energy or power, but rather, all of its strength and power is now under the control of its master. Now the horse has a sense of purpose and direction.

A Product of Brokenness

First, true meekness is a product of brokenness. The picture of taming wild animals works well in the spiritual realm also. The horse's wild spirit needs to be broken so that it will be useful. When it is broken, it becomes meek, not weak. The wild horse, once uncontrollable, now yields its will and gives control to the rider.

In a person, meekness is yielding control of one's personal will and giving it to God. Think about Jacob. Before he was defeated and broken in his wrestling match with the angel of the Lord, he was resistant. But, when he was defeated, he submitted his will and turned control of his life over to God (Genesis 32:22–32).

Regardless of the circumstances that lead to brokenness, the one important thing is that we leave the experience having acquired meekness. Watch how the first two Beatitudes work with this: When we are broken and begin to mourn, the result is meekness. It is a natural result of dependence on God.

Merely trying to be meek doesn't work. No sermon on being meek will make us magically meek. Rather, it comes by realizing that we are dependent on God for salvation and then humbly submitting to His teaching and His shaping of our lives.

Paul shared the value of meekness in his admonition in Galatians 6:1–2. He advised the Galatians in this way: "Brethren, if a man is overtaken in any trespass, you who are spiritual restore such a one in a spirit of gentleness, considering yourself lest you also be tempted. Bear one another's burdens, and so fulfill the law of Christ."

Gentle, Not Spineless

Second, brokenness that creates gentleness does not produce spinelessness. When we become meek, we do not turn into cowardly, wimpy people. In fact, it is just the opposite. A meek person is no longer flesh-driven, but spirit-directed. We have the strength to overcome hardships, to love difficult people, and to tirelessly follow our Father's instructions. We stop depending on our own abilities and tap in to the never-ceasing ocean of God's resources.

Think about Jesus' holy anger. In Matthew 11:29, He said, "I am gentle and humble in heart" (NIV). He was a gentle breeze and a soothing medicine to those who had been beaten and battered by life. But this same meek, mild Jesus, when faced with superficial and self-righteous Pharisees, rose up with bold authority. Mark 3:5 says that when the Pharisees tried to stop Him from healing a man's hand on the Sabbath, "He looked around at them in anger" (NIV). When faced with people who had turned the Temple into a gift shop, Jesus overturned tables and drove out those who were seeking to cheat honest worshippers. Jesus spoke out against injustice because those men were angering God.

Meekness Is Not Weakness

Becoming meek does not mean that we become people

without conviction. It doesn't mean that we will never have to take a stand. It just means that our strength and power are under the control of God. It is when God's truth is reviled that the Lion of Judah pounces. It is hard sometimes to tell the difference between holy anger and a temper tantrum. How can we distinguish between the two?

> But when you do good and suffer, if you take it patiently, this is commendable before God. For to this you were called, because Christ also suffered for us, leaving us an example, that you should follow His steps: "Who committed no sin, nor was deceit found in His mouth"; who, when He was reviled, did not revile in return; when He suffered, He did not threaten, but committed Himself to Him who judges righteously...
>
> **—1 Peter 2:20b–23**

You see, when Jesus was offended, defamed, and spoken evil of, "He made no threats" (1 Peter 2:23 NIV). He didn't care if people spoke against Him. We should not take this to mean that He didn't feel pained when He was defamed. I think this hurt Him deeply. No doubt part of His pain came from the fact that the people whom He had come to save despised Him. I think this pain may have been worse than the physical pain He went through. He had been rejected.

When the Pharisees shut the door on the Kingdom, Jesus moved. When the Temple of God was defamed, He cleared the Temple using a whip. When God was made to look like something He wasn't, He moved. But when He was attacked on a personal level, He did not react.

How should we respond when people pick us apart and hurt us? Should we say, "That doesn't bother me. I am Jesus' doormat"? Our feelings are going to get hurt, and we shouldn't be in denial when it happens. As Peter so wisely wrote in 1 Peter 2:23, Jesus "entrusted himself to him who judges justly" (NIV). We must trust that God will exalt us and defend us when we are unjustly treated. God will straighten things out at the right time.

The Meek Are Teachable

Therefore, lay aside all filthiness and overflow of wicked-ness, and receive with meekness the implanted word, which is able to save your souls.
—James 1:21

A meek person is teachable. A teachable spirit should be a way of life. Meek people come to the Bible, to church, and to everyday life with a humble attitude. They recognize that they are sinners and that they need to be taught a better way of life. People like this grow by leaps and bounds because they acknowledge their brokenness and are thirsty to learn how to change.

Nothing is more obnoxious than a proud, arrogant person sharing his or her faith. And nothing makes us want to learn more about Jesus than a person who admits his failings and meekly shares what he or she has learned. When we are meek, we are teachable, and this meekness helps others want to learn more about the God we serve.

The call to meekness is not a call to weakness. Meekness is submitting your strengths to Someone who can put them to greater use. It's impossible to abide with God and not be submitting to His plan for our lives. Recognizing our sin leads us to mourn for it, which prompts us to humbly reach out to God for direction. Our ego and our self-righteousness disappear, and we draw closer to abiding with Jesus.

Chapter Four Questions

Question: Define the biblical concept of meekness. How does it differ from our modern perception? What are some word-pictures that describe meekness?

_____

_____

_____

_____

_____

_____

_____

_____

_____

_____

_____

Question: How did Jesus demonstrate and model meekness?

_____

_____

_____

_____

_____

_____

_____

_____

_____

_____

_____

Action: In Numbers 12:3, Moses is described as the meekest man on earth. Study the life of Moses and chart times when he excelled—and a few times he failed—in displaying meekness.

Journal: Meditate on Matthew 5:5 and Matthew 11:28–30. How can you learn meekness from Jesus? How will walking in *His* power change your interactions with others?

Chapter Four Notes

CHAPTER FIVE

Those Who Hunger and Thirst

Blessed are those who hunger and thirst for righteousness,
for they shall be filled.

—Matthew 5:6

Greek mythology tells the tragic story of Tantalus, a son of Zeus, who angered the gods by stealing their divine food. As punishment, he was condemned to the depths of Tartarus, where he would forever stand in a pool of water with a hanging vine above him. Whenever Tantalus would dip to drink from the pool, the water would recede just out of touch of his lips. Whenever he reached for the fruit, it would retreat just out of reach of his fingers.

His punishment was eternal thirst and hunger. No matter how hard he tried, he would never be able to quench his thirst or satisfy his hunger.

Fortunately for the believer, our heavenly Father isn't so cruel. He promises living water that quenches our thirst, and spiritual food that satisfies the hunger of our souls.

The essence of hungering for righteousness is having a sacred desire for identity in Christ alone. This hunger develops an intimacy with Christ that is the foundation of our faith.

I think this is a Beatitude to which most of us can relate easier than the others, because we understand what it is like to be hungry and thirsty. What separates some people from others is not that some hunger and thirst while others don't. What distinguishes us is where we choose to "eat and drink." What separates us can be discovered by what we define as our "bread and water." What do we need, and where do we look to have our core needs met?

Hungering and thirsting are descriptions of a driving force, a strong desire, or a single-minded ambition. Whatever I hunger and thirst for is what I genuinely desire. Hungry, thirsty people are highly motivated.

Think of this in the biological sense. You hunger for food and thirst for water. These two things are essential for life. Without food or water, you will die. Now, carry that over to the spiritual side. You hunger and thirst for things that you have identified as vital to your sense of purpose and meaning. If you don't have them, you die spiritually. Life will be meaningless.

Life Essentials

We all have things that drive our actions. Some of these things are simple wants or preferences, and they come and go. However, we are all driven by desires deep down inside of us that can't be ignored. Sure, we can wait if we're hungry or thirsty for a little while, but eventually we will need to eat or drink.

I call these "life essentials" because they are necessary for our emotional and mental survival. Life essentials all need to be met in Christ. When we start looking elsewhere, we create idols and fall into sinful habits.

For most of us, one life essential is love. We yearn to be loved for who we are. We want to be intimately known and cared for. When we allow God to meet this need, both through His love and the love of people He's placed in our lives, we feel spiritually full.

But when we try to meet this need on our own, we are always disappointed. The people we choose to love us can't do it perfectly, like God can. We turn to fantasies of perfect love, to pornography, to food, or to distraction. We read romance novels and watch movies about people falling in love, and we wonder what they're doing right and what we're doing wrong.

In the same way, we chase after all sorts of heart-level desires: success, comfort, approval, power, relief from pain. When we try to satiate these on our own, we will fail. Life essentials are met by God when we run to Him and allow Him to provide for us.

What are your life essentials? While this answer will vary from person to person, I think we all share a few common life essentials. We each have a hunger for meaning and a thirst for a sense of value. We share a desire to be loved and to love. We all long for happiness and fulfillment. These are common for everyone, no matter where you are in life.

A Mouthful of Dust

The things most people turn to for satisfying their hunger and thirst simply fail to deliver. We often lack a sense of meaning and purpose. The prophet Amos described us as, "These who pant after the dust of the earth" (Amos 2:7 NASB). Amos looked around at everyone and declared that they were eating and drinking what amounted to a mouthful of dust. All of them were eating what could not satisfy their souls.

Throughout human history, people have indulged in meaningless/ungodly things and activities to try to fill the void that God intended to be filled only through His righteousness. We are not blessed if we hunger and thirst for things other than righteousness, because we will never be fulfilled. The yearning to have our life essentials sated will have us on an endless search until we come to Christ.

> *Jesus answered and said to her, "Whoever drinks of this water will thirst again, but whoever drinks of the water that I shall give him will never thirst. But the water that I shall give him will become in him a fountain of water springing up into everlasting life."*
> **—John 4:13-14**

Life essentials are like an appetite, in that they need to be met over and over again. When we find ourselves struggling with sin in one of these areas, we often delude ourselves with the lie of "just one more time." Appetites don't go away forever. It's sort of like this: No matter how good your cheeseburger is, you'll be hungry again in a few hours. Appetites for sin work the same way. Whatever you do to "scratch the itch" now won't satisfy the need for long; it will quickly become dust in our mouths.

The American Dream

We're incredibly blessed to live in a country where we can pursue our dreams. This freedom allows us to live in the kind of house we want, to create the type of family we desire, and to have the career we wish to pursue. It's easy to get wrapped up in the pursuit of these desires and to believe that, once we achieve them, we'll stop hungering for more.

What people often do is just get a bigger house or bigger boat. Don't get me wrong: There is nothing wrong with houses, boats, or other material things. But we are in trouble if we expect those things to fulfill our deepest needs. Nothing will ever be good or big enough. It is dust. Let the words of Solomon sink into your heart as you read these verses from Ecclesiastes. Solomon had wisdom, wealth, houses, land, and more earthly pleasures than anyone alive at that time, yet it was all a mouthful of dust.

I said in my heart, "Come now, I will test you with mirth; therefore, enjoy pleasure"; but surely, this also was vanity. I said of laughter—"Madness!"; and of mirth, "What does it accomplish?" I searched in my heart how to gratify my flesh with wine, while guiding my heart with wisdom, and how to lay hold on folly, till I might see what was good for the sons of men to do under heaven all the days of their lives.

I made my works great, I built myself houses, and planted

*myself vineyards. I made myself gardens and orchards, and
I planted all kinds of fruit trees in them. I made myself water pools from which to water the growing trees of the
grove. I acquired male and female servants, and had servants born in my house. Yes, I had greater possessions of
herds and flocks than all who were in Jerusalem before me.
I also gathered for myself silver and gold and the special
treasures of kings and of the provinces. I acquired male
and female singers, the delights of the sons of men, and mu-
sical instruments of all kinds.*

*So I became great and excelled more than all who were be-
fore me in Jerusalem. Also, my wisdom remained with me.*

*Whatever my eyes desired I did not keep from them. I did
not withhold my heart from any pleasure, for my heart re-
joiced in all my labor; and this was my reward from all my
labor. Then I looked on all the works that my hands had
done and on the labor in which I had toiled; and indeed, all
was vanity and grasping for the wind. There was no profit
under the sun.*

—Ecclesiastes 2:1–11

The Things for Which We Hunger

If you're not feeding off of the "American Dream,"
then what are you feeding off of? Maybe it's status, success, career, family, or education that feeds you? Many
people use one or several of these to feed on or find purpose and value. Are you feeding off of a hurt, a habit, or a
hang-up? Something that is a coping mechanism that
never addresses the core issue of unrighteousness in your
life? Many Christians use religious activity. We might
feed off of our performance in ministry. You may connect
your satisfaction with how many services you participate
in during a week. You may self-righteously serve people

as a means to be accepted by God. Someone who is strung out on drugs has the same core needs as the religious person trying to please God her own way. The question still remains: *What do you look to for satisfaction?*

> *Has a nation changed its gods, which are not gods? But My people have changed their Glory for what does not profit. Be astonished, O heavens, at this, and be horribly afraid; be very desolate," says the LORD. "For My people have committed two evils: they have forsaken Me, the fountain of living waters, and hewn themselves cisterns—broken cisterns that can hold no water.*
> **—Jeremiah 2:11–13**

Jeremiah, under the inspiration of God, spoke this word over the nation of Israel. He was astonished that anyone would allow a counterfeit in place of the real God. He was declaring that they had the glory of God and the pure righteousness from Him, and yet they chose the inferior.

Do you know what a cistern is? A cistern is reservoir that holds water. It's not quite as bad as a sewer drain, but not far off. The cisterns were used to gather rainwater for irrigation and cleaning, but not usually for drinking. That rainwater would be full of dirt and every nasty thing it picked up along the way until it settled in the cisterns. Many times, animals would get in the cisterns and die and infect the water.

God was telling His people that they had rejected His pure righteousness. Instead, they were depending on their own righteousness, which was dirty and full of inadequacies.

It is hard to imagine how anyone in their right mind

would choose to drink from a cistern if they had a spring or fountain of fresh pure water, and yet, spiritually, we do it all the time. We have the pure water of God available to us, and yet we create our own self-righteous cisterns that are not refreshing or sanitary, and we indulge in them.

Two Kinds of Righteousness

We must ask the question: How can this hunger and thirst be satisfied? Matthew 5:6 says that "those who hunger and thirst for righteousness … *will be filled*" (NIV). Then, we must ask, "What kind of righteousness are we to hunger for?"

First of all, we must define *righteousness*. When you are born again, God pronounces you righteous through Christ. This means that you are acquitted of the guilt of sin that was against you. You are innocent and no longer subject to the penalty of sin. Christ took that for you. You cannot be any more righteous than you are when you're born again.

However, sanctification, transformation, and holiness are a process. As you grow in your abiding relationship with Christ, He transforms your desires into godly ones.

Unfortunately, the word *righteous* in the Bible is translated in various ways, which can generate confusion. It's true that *righteousness* refers to moral or ethical living or to a lack of sin—but such definitions require further clarity. When the Bible uses the word *righteous* in the context of talking about your process of sanctification, transformation, and holiness, it is referring to your actions as a fruit of who you are in Christ. (We will explore this more in chapter 7, regarding purity of heart.)

When the Bible describes your right standing with God as righteous, it means you're innocent, without guilt, and acquitted. Do you see the difference? You are already pronounced righteous no matter what you do for God. However, when you live in your identity in Christ, this righteousness affects your choices as He transforms you into His image and causes you to live righteously.

The Bible talks about two kinds of righteousness. We find in Matthew 5:20 the "righteousness of Pharisees," a self-declared righteousness. Then, in Philippians 3:9, we find the righteousness of Christ, which is Savior-granted.

Many people give the Pharisees a hard time, but they were actually trying to reinstate Jewish customs and the Law in order to create a "righteous" people. What ended up happening is what happens with all of us—they became self-righteous. They assumed that they were better than the other Jews because they had knowledge and outward alignment to the law. They started out with good intentions but ended up becoming bound by something that fell short of God's best.

Theologian D. A. Carson explains that authentic, biblical Christianity goes beyond "rules and regulations" to produce "transformed men and women—men and women who, because of the power of the Spirit of God, enjoy regenerated natures. We want to please God, we want to be holy, we want to confess Jesus is Lord. In short, the sins we once loved we learn to fear and hate, the obedience and holiness we once despised we now hunger for."[10]

The apostle Paul knew well the allure of self-righteousness, as he explained in this brief autobiographical sketch from his letter to the Philippians:

> *If anyone else thinks he may have confidence in the flesh, I more so: circumcised the eighth day, of the stock of Israel, of the tribe of Benjamin, a Hebrew of the Hebrews; concerning the law, a Pharisee; concerning zeal, persecuting the church; concerning the righteousness which is in the law, blameless.*
> **—Philippians 3:4–6**

This is quite an impressive list of religious accomplishments! Paul was on the "Who's Who" list of Pharisees. He had been trained under one of the greatest leaders of the synagogue at that time. He was a Roman citizen, which afforded him rights that many other Jewish people didn't have, and he had a zeal that put others in his sect to shame. There was not a flaw in his credentials.

But one day, on a journey to persecute Christians, his perspective changed. He realized he was eating dust. He learned the truth about Jesus, the very One he was persecuting. Paul realized that the righteousness needed to quench his thirst came only from Christ. He needed Christ's righteousness given to him by grace through faith. That is the true water and food for our soul. It's the only thing that satisfies.

Immediately following his list of accomplishments in verse 4–6, Paul went on to say:

> *But what things were gain to me, these I have counted loss for Christ. Yet indeed I also count all things loss for the excellence of the knowledge of Christ Jesus my Lord, for*

*whom I have suffered the loss of all things, and count them
as rubbish, that I may gain Christ and be found in Him, not
having my own righteousness, which is from the law, but
that which is through faith in Christ, the righteousness
which is from God by faith; that I may know Him and the
power of His resurrection, and the fellowship of His suffer-
ings, being conformed to His death...*
—Philippians 3:7–10

Many years ago, I saw a skit in church in which two
men were sitting in the waiting room to get into heaven.
The first man had a duffel bag that held evidence of all of
the things he did right. He pulled out trophies, certificates,
and ribbons that proved how much money he gave, his
perfect attendance at church, and even his excellent driving record.

The second man had none of these things, and though
he listened attentively as the first man listed his accomplishments, he confidently assured the first man that none
of these things would help. And, sure enough, the call was
made for the second man to enter heaven, leaving the first
behind with his bag of good things.

The second man knew that he wasn't good enough on
his own, that his good deeds didn't outweigh his sin, and
that the only way to find freedom was through Jesus
Christ. He examined his heart and knew that his life essentials would always leave him thirsting for more. And
this man humbly bowed his heart to Jesus. His spiritual
hunger and thirst drew him to God, where he could abide
constantly, his needs being met every moment of every
day.

Take your example from the second man and pursue

your hunger and thirst into a deep, abiding relationship with Jesus. You can find a more in-depth discussion of the essence of this beatitude in my book *Abiding in Identity*.[11]

But it comes down to this: allow His righteousness to be what you hunger and thirst for and you will be fully satisfied.

WORKBOOK

Chapter Five Questions

Question: What are the life essentials for which you hunger? Where and how do you seek to fill these needs apart from Christ?

_____

_____

_____

_____

_____

_____

_____

_____

_____

_____

_____

_____

Question: What are the two kinds of righteousness? How can you embrace and grow in Christ's righteousness?

_____

_____

_____

_____

_____

_____

_____

_____

_____

_____

_____

Action: Divide a piece of paper into two columns. On one side write "The American Dream promises..." and list the benefits that come to mind. On the other side write "Christ's kingdom promises..." and list the scripturally based blessings He offers. Then examine how you spend your time, money, talents, and affections, to determine whether you're hungering for the American Dream or for Christ's kingdom.

Journal: Meditate on Matthew 5:6 and Philippians 3:4–10. Where are you finding your identity? How are you growing in intimacy with Christ?

Chapter Five Notes

_____

_____

_____

_____

_____

_____

_____

_____

_____

_____

_____

_____

_____

_____

_____

_____

_____

_____

_____

_____

_____

_____

_____

_____

CHAPTER SIX

The Merciful

Blessed are the merciful, for they shall obtain mercy.
—Matthew 5:7

In Matthew 18, Peter approaches Jesus with the question, "Lord, how many times shall I forgive my brother or sister who sins against me? Up to seven times?" (verse 21 NIV).

Peter was expecting Jesus to say that there would be an end to the mercy we're to extend to others. Jesus' response, however, was just as surprising then as it is now.

"I tell you, not seven times, but seventy-seven times" (verse 22 NIV).

What is your response when you've been wronged by someone, especially by someone who repeatedly harms you and shows no remorse for their actions? Do you continue to extend mercy, or do you ever reach the point where enough is just enough?

What Is Mercy?

The essence of mercy expresses the fact that when we receive the mercy of God, our natural response should be to extend mercy to others.

There's a common expression I like a lot. It says, "Grace is when you get what you don't deserve. Mercy is when you don't get what you do deserve."

Think about the people who were listening as Jesus gave His Sermon on the Mount. It was a rough-looking bunch of people, wasn't it? Imagine they were longing for what He would say next after He introduced broken, mourning, meek, and hungry conversations.

In Paul's words:

> Brothers and sisters, think of what you were when you were called. Not many of you were wise by human standards; not many were influential; many were not of noble birth.
> **—1 Corinthians 1:26** (NIV)

This group does not sound like much, but they were the ones whom God called. This is a powerful Kingdom principle: It matters less about where you start and more about your heart. God can take anyone willing to come His way and use them to bring glory to His name.

Being merciful is aiding the afflicted, helping the wretched, and rescuing the miserable. In the Bible, the word *mercy* points in two directions. First, it can refer to a kindness shown to someone in need. Second, it can refer to a punishment withheld from a guilty person.

Mercy was not valued in Jesus' day as much as it is in ours. The Romans were merciless, and that ruthlessness aided them as they conquered neighboring people. The Pharisees studied the Law, which was clear on the importance of showing mercy. They knew what God commanded along these lines, but they were unable to fulfill it. Perhaps they spent so much of their time meeting the letter of the law that they looked down on those who seemed to focus more on God's mercy than on working their way to external perfection.

Merciful Acts Versus Merciful People

The Pharisees were definitely capable of merciful acts. But we must make a distinction: They were not merciful people. Do you see the difference? The Pharisees could prepare themselves ahead of time to do a merciful act. But doing a single merciful act isn't the same as having a merciful spirit.

Here is the reason that people like the Pharisees are incapable of being merciful: Mercy and grace don't come out of proud, self-righteous people. Generally speaking, rigidity, intolerance, judgmental attitudes, and condemnation flow out of them, but very little mercy.

The people through whom mercy will flow are people to whom mercy has come. To put in another way, people who know they need mercy, and then get it, will show it. Those who know what it feels like when mercy comes have experienced its healing power. Therefore, these people extend mercy to others.

A Biblical Example of Mercy

But he, wanting to justify himself, said to Jesus, "And who is my neighbor?"

Then Jesus answered and said: "A certain man went down from Jerusalem to Jericho, and fell among thieves, who stripped him of his clothing, wounded him, and departed, leaving him half dead. Now by chance a certain priest came down that road. And when he saw him, he passed by on the other side. Likewise a Levite, when he arrived at the place, came and looked, and passed by on the other side. But a certain Samaritan, as he journeyed, came where he was. And when he saw him, he had compassion. So he went to him and bandaged his wounds, pouring on oil and wine; and he set him on his own animal, brought him to an inn, and took care of him. On the next day, when he departed, he took out two denarii, gave them to the innkeeper, and said to him, 'Take care of him; and whatever more you spend, when I come again, I will repay you.' So which of these three do you think was neighbor to him who fell among the thieves?"

And he said, "He who showed mercy on him."

Then Jesus said to him, "Go and do likewise."
—Luke 10:29–37

Here is a man who was beaten and left to die on the side of the road. A priest and a Levite had both seen this man in need, but they acted like they didn't see him. The Samaritan had mercy on this man and immediately came to his aid. The Samaritan picked him up and took him to a place to recover from his wounds. He even paid all the hospital bills. Why did he stop, but not the others?

Here is why I think he stopped and the others didn't. He knew what it was like to be in the gutter and left for dead himself. He had experienced something the priest and Levite never had; rejection and ridicule. The Samaritans were referred to as "half-breeds." The Jews simply didn't accept them, and they were considered less than human. So, this man who stopped to help could relate to what it felt like to be trashed and left for dead. It was firsthand experience for him. He knew what it felt like to be in need of mercy and to receive it.

Here is the catch: I don't believe that everyone who has mercy extended to them receives it. Mercy doesn't work as healing power for those who don't feel like they need it in the first place. Let's look at two kinds of people who find it hard to receive mercy.

The Self-Righteous

Rachel was a good student. She studied and worked hard. She practiced volleyball and softball on the evenings and weekends and made the high school varsity teams while she was still in middle school. In college, she continued her string of achievements and completed a law degree with honors.

Now, as an adult, Rachel struggles to see why she needs God. When she looks at herself, Rachel thinks she's doing pretty well. Sure, she's not perfect, but she isn't a terrible sinner, either, right? Surely the good things she does will outweigh the bad.

Rachel's struggle is with self-righteousness. Self-righteous people don't understand God's mercy, simply because they feel that they only get what they deserved. They believe that an easy life is something they've earned.

Some of them don't even feel they need mercy because they believe they are already pretty close to perfect.

Those Who Are Ashamed

Donna got pregnant before she was married and had an abortion. Almost instantly, she regretted it. This act drove her back to God, but she was unable to accept His mercy. Donna felt that what she had done was so awful that accepting God's forgiveness would mean that she hadn't shown the depths of her regret. She didn't want an easy way out. Sorrow over her lost child was the payment that Donna demanded of herself. She refused to extend herself the mercy that God had already given her.

People who are full of shame find it hard to receive mercy. Like the self-righteous, the ashamed need mercy, too. The difference is that self-righteous people feel like they don't need mercy or that they've earned it, while the ashamed can't accept that mercy is possible. They hear about grace and mercy and the fact they have an unpayable debt, and it paralyzes them. When you tell them that God has already paid off their debt, they just can't let that forgiveness in.

They are incapable of letting it in because of two beliefs that they hold: "I have to deserve this," and "I certainly don't deserve this." The person struggling with shame will have the same struggle as a self-righteous person in accepting free gifts. Both believe they have to earn it. But people who are ashamed never feel clean or complete.

The Gift

By definition, we cannot earn grace and mercy. It is a free gift (Ephesians 2:8–9). In a sense, both the self-righteous and the ashamed are right: We don't deserve it. But God longs to gift us lavishly with His mercy and grace (Ephesians 1:6).

The hope for both the self-righteous and the ashamed is that God is calling them to draw closer to Him. He calls us all to come near to Jesus so that we can understand our sin and learn about the bottomless mercy that our heavenly Father has for us.

We can't give what we don't have. If we come to a place where we know we need mercy and receive it, then we will have it to give. When we realize that we need to be accepted by God, we will be accepting of others. But, unless we've come to that place, we won't have it to give.

When we are in proximity with Christ, abiding in Him, our hearts are able to hear when God calls us to extend mercy to someone, or even to ourselves. As we understand the hurt that we ourselves have caused, then we are able to forgive those who hurt us. As we learn about the patience that God has with us, we can overlook annoyances and frustrations that pop up in our own lives.

The unlovable, difficult people in our lives become our missions. We begin to pray for them, to speak to them kindly, and to not be embarrassed to count these people as our friends. The "cool people" who have it all together might be the ones we want to be seen with, but often the messy, awkward, needy people are the ones whom God wants us to love. Because I understand the mercy that He showed me, I can befriend that guy from work, even though his hygiene is lacking and he speaks with a lisp. I can allow my daughter to be friends with the girl with the single mom who doesn't have time to teach her good manners. I don't have to have it all together, because God gave me mercy, and I can allow the people around me to feel free to not have it all together, either.

It is through this abiding relationship with God that we receive the mercy we need and become living examples to others of the merciful God whom we serve.

WORKBOOK

Chapter Six Questions

Question: What is the connection between receiving mercy and showing mercy? Who are the people who have the easiest time extending mercy to others?

_____

_____

_____

_____

_____

_____

_____

_____

_____

_____

_____

Question: What are the two greatest hindrances to receiving God's mercy? Which one do you find to be the most challenging in your own life?

_____

_____

_____

_____

_____

_____

_____

_____

_____

_____

Action: Plan an "act of mercy" this week, and ask God to give you a heart of mercy for those to whom you minister because of the mercy He has shown you. If you do not have a friend, relative, or acquaintance in special need of mercy right now, consider volunteering at a homeless shelter, crisis pregnancy center, children's home, or immigrant/refugee ministry.

Journal: Meditate on Matthew 5:7 and the story of Good Samaritan in Luke 10:29–37. Have you seen your need for and accepted God's mercy in your own life? How do you extend His mercy to others?

Chapter Six Notes

_____

_____

_____

_____

_____

_____

_____

_____

_____

_____

_____

_____

_____

_____

_____

_____

_____

_____

_____

_____

CHAPTER SEVEN

The Pure in Heart

Blessed are the pure in heart, for they shall see God.
—Matthew 5:8

The essence of a pure heart is a heart that has been sifted and cleansed and has its affection fixed firmly on God.

God looks at you with love in His eyes. He created you in His very image and likeness but sin marred that, which distorted the image. When you were born again, God restored the marred image and re-created you in newness of life. However, you look in the mirror and see the sinful person instead of the person into whom He has transformed you. But God is saying, "Look in the mirror of the Spirit of God and see that I truly created you in My likeness." This is such a powerful conversation that we must not gloss over it if we are going to abide in Christ and find our identity in Him.

God desires us to be broken in spirit and to have the

beggarly dependence upon Him that will produce in us a mourning over our sin, and then ultimately repentance. This produces in us a meekness that is a soothing medicine and a gentle breeze—and a controlled power. That, in turn, produces in us an ability to both receive and give mercy. It produces a hungering and a thirsting, not after external religious things, but after the very righteousness of God.

Would you have the nerve to say that you have a pure heart before God? You're not alone if you aren't quick to jump up and holler, "Yes!"

How dare we say that we have a pure heart before God! Doesn't the Bible say that the heart is evil and wicked—that we are sinful people, and that only God is holy (Jeremiah 17:9)?

Yes, those are two true statements, but they aren't the whole story. This chapter will focus on what it looks like to have a pure heart before a holy, loving, and pure God.

Is the Heart Evil?

The heart is deceitful above all things, and desperately wicked; who can know it?
—Jeremiah 17:9

Who can say, "I have made my heart clean, I am pure from my sin"?
—Proverbs 20:9

To be honest, I have been amazed over the years how

much misunderstanding surrounds the topic of our evil hearts. This is one area in which Satan has deceived so many in the Church. I have heard the verses above quoted over and over as an excuse as to why people cannot be held to a standard of holiness.

I argue that, not only can you have a pure heart, but that it is a requirement of a disciple. Not only can you be holy, but God expects it of you. Part of the gift of redemption is a pure heart. Living in your identity in Christ comes with purity of heart. Don't allow anyone to deter you from what God's Word says you can have or keep you from walking in it.

As much as the Bible tells us there is not one righteous and that the heart is evil, it also tells us that in Christ we can have a new heart and walk in the righteousness of God. What is this apparent contradiction all about? We know that sin keeps the unredeemed, human heart desiring things that are contrary to God. Now, let's examine what the new birth does in the human heart.

Defining the Terms

The best way I can describe this is to say that your spirit makes you who you are—it's what the Bible calls the inner person (2 Corinthians 4:16; 1 Peter 3:4; Ephesians 3:16). You have a soul that is comprised of your will, emotions, and understanding. All of this is housed in this earthly tent, the body (2 Corinthians 5:1). The spirit and soul are intimately connected and will exist forever. Many times, they are used interchangeably in conversation, but they are very different.

This fallen body is temporary, and when your spirit and soul are removed, your body will be lifeless. If you were to see me driving down the road and wave to me, would you yell out to your other neighbors, "There goes Nate's car"? No, you would simply say, "There goes Nate." This is the same way with our makeup. Your body simply houses the real you.

Heart, Soul, and Body

Let's look at a handful of scriptures that define the different aspects of our threefold, or three-part, nature. This is very important for you to learn in your life with Christ. To live in the fullness of your identity, you must learn to understand each aspect of your nature and navigate as the Bible directs.

Your human nature comprises a threefold existence:

> *Now may the God of peace Himself sanctify you completely; and may your whole spirit, soul, and body be preserved blameless at the coming of our Lord Jesus Christ.*
> **—1 Thessalonians 5:23**

> *For the word of God is living and powerful, and sharper than any two-edged sword, piercing even to the division of soul and spirit, and of joints and marrow, and is a discerner of the thoughts and intents of the heart.*
> **—Hebrews 4:12**

Your inner person is where God resides:

> *The spirit of a man is the lamp of the LORD, searching all the inner depths of his heart.*
> **—Proverbs 20:27**

Obedience comes from your inner person:

> *But God be thanked that though you were slaves of sin, yet you obeyed from the heart that form of doctrine to which you were delivered.*
> **—Romans 6:17**

When you are born again, God circumcises your heart and gives you a new heart because you are a new creation in Christ:

> *But he is a Jew who is one inwardly; and circumcision is that of the heart, in the Spirit, not in the letter; whose praise is not from men but from God.*
> **—Romans 2:29**

> *Therefore, if anyone is in Christ, he is a new creation; old things have passed away; behold, all things have become new.*
> **—2 Corinthians 5:17**

Your flesh is dying, but your inner person should be renewed daily:

Therefore we do not lose heart. Even though our outward man is perishing, yet the inward man is being renewed day by day.
—2 Corinthians 4:16

Before we are saved, our hearts were wicked, our minds were evil, and our sinful nature led us to do what we pleased. When we were born again, our hearts were changed and became alive to Christ. We became new creations. The Holy Spirit does a re-creative work, and indeed we are now different. This is an immediate change that is glorious and amazing. We are empowered for godly living through the Holy Spirit.

And do not present your members as instruments of unrighteousness to sin, but present yourselves to God as being alive from the dead, and your members as instruments of righteousness to God. For sin shall not have dominion over you, for you are not under law but under grace.
—Romans 6:13–14

When you are born again, if you go and look in the mirror, do you notice any physical changes? If you had gray hair, you still have gray hair. If you were tall or short, none of that changed. The new birth is not a physical change; it's an inner change. The Bible is clear that the sinful nature wants to indulge in fleshly things. You must learn to crucify your sinful desires, or these tendencies will dominate your life. Sin should not dominate you any longer.

At the same time, you still have a mind and emotions that have been trained to obey the demands of your desire.

Every decision and action you made prior to rebirth was indulged in self-centered, sinful tendencies.

Many new believers are frustrated because they still feel the draw of the old nature, with its selfish thought patterns (Romans 7:13–25). This is all normal until you begin to allow the Holy Spirit to change you from the inside out. This transformation goes against everything you have ever known and experienced, and it can be painful.

Biblical Transformation

Remember when we talked about the taming of the wild horse in chapter 4? Think about the changes in thinking, habits, and intuition that would need to occur for this horse to be gentled. Before, he was responsible for finding food, water, and shelter. He ran where he wanted, protected himself when he was in danger, and could leap about wildly whenever he felt the urge.

As the horse is trained, he must learn to trust that his new master will provide him with a safe living environment. He is taught how to wear a restrictive bridle and to respond to commands. No longer can he buck and leap whenever he wants. It's not an easy process, is it?

As we become a "new creation," as 2 Corinthians 5:17 describes it, we must die to our sin natures, change our thinking, and begin responding to the Holy Spirit's promptings. Over time, this process of transformation and renewal of the mind will change us into the image of Christ (Romans 8:29).

What a powerful expression of transformation. God has given us complete liberty by imparting the Holy Spirit to us. He then proceeds to transform us into His image from one degree of glory to the next. In a true abiding relationship with Christ, this transformation will continue on an incremental basis and reveal more and more of God to us. At the same time, this will produce a change in our old man into Christ's likeness and image.

Learning to hear the Holy Spirit doesn't happen overnight. Just like a wild horse doesn't become docile the moment it steps into a stable, we don't flip a switch and suddenly have a transformed soul on a whim. Studying the Bible, being mentored by people who are spiritually mature, learning to self-feed on and apply God's Word in our lives, spending time in prayer, and fasting are all some of the ways in which God works to transform our souls.

Living with a Pure Heart

Although it seems unattainable, the necessity of a pure heart is undeniable. It is not just a suggestion. No, these Beatitudes are emphatic. Jesus is saying, "Blessed are the pure in heart, for they will see God." Taken another way, that could mean that those that don't have pure hearts won't see God.

A pure heart is undivided, unmixed, unadulterated, sifted, genuine, and real, with no added mixture or element.

I think that one crucial element of having a pure heart is entering into an intimate abiding relationship with God. Imagine what would happen to a wild horse who is beaten by its master or isn't provided with good food. If the master was rough with the horse, it would never really become tamed. It might eventually obey out of fear, but the horse will still hold on to that wildness and possibly be a danger to the master and itself.

Jesus wants us to know that Kingdom life is a relational matter of the heart. And we can all get excited about that for one reason: We really do love God down deep in our hearts. We may stumble and fall at times, but the bottom line is that, in our hearts, we have a passion for Jesus and for the things of God. With all of our inconsistencies, there is still a determination to love Jesus with all of our hearts.

This was a problem for people both in the Old and the New Testaments. The one thing God cared about more than anything else was being deeply loved. And, this was the one thing people found most difficult to recognize.

When you think about it, it isn't hard to understand why. When I follow rules, I don't have to worry about my attitude. Imagine your preteen daughter emptying the dishwasher the way you asked her to, grumbling and rolling her eyes the whole time.

It's the same way with God. If I distance myself from a relationship with Him, I can conduct business ethically, not cheat on my wife, and go to church every Sunday while still enjoying my secret sin. I'm following the rules I want to follow, right? Therefore, I can excuse myself from being obedient in every area. When I don't bother to be close enough to my heavenly Father to hear Him call me out on these issues, I don't have to look too closely at myself.

A Pure Heart Requires Faith

So, if actions alone don't create a pure heart, then what does? This is a question even the apostles had to sit and consider.

> *Now the apostles and elders came together to consider this matter. And when there had been much dispute, Peter rose up and said to them: "Men and brethren, you know that a good while ago God chose among us, that by my mouth the Gentiles should hear the word of the gospel and believe. So God, who knows the heart, acknowledged them by giving them the Holy Spirit, just as He did to us, and made no distinction between us and them, purifying their hearts by faith.*
>
> *—Acts 15:6–9*

First, a pure heart is received by faith. We see in Acts 15 that a debate had arisen in the early church. The problem had to do with the status of the new Gentile believers who had not yet been circumcised. Some were implying that the uncircumcised couldn't be saved. Peter answered them above with the reminder that God purified them in their hearts by faith, not by the work of circumcision (Acts 15:1–29).

If a pure heart is received by faith, then we must ask, "Faith in what?" We can't clean our own hearts. But by faith, we can experience the cleansing power of Jesus. We can ask for this pure heart. We can let God's grace in and receive it. We have clearly seen this in the progression of the Beatitudes.

"This is the covenant that I will make with them after those days, says the LORD: *I will put my laws into their hearts, and in their minds, I will write them," then He adds, "Their sins and their lawless deeds I will remember no more." Now where there is remission of these, there is no longer an offering for sin.*

—Hebrews 10:16–18

Then I will sprinkle clean water on you, and you shall be clean; I will cleanse you from all your filthiness and from all your idols. I will give you a new heart and put a new spirit within you; I will take the heart of stone out of your flesh and give you a heart of flesh. I will put My Spirit within you and cause you to walk in My statutes, and you will keep My judgments and do them.

—Ezekiel 36:25–27

A Pure Heart Requires the Holy Spirit

Second, the pure heart is implanted by the Holy Spirit. When, by faith, we receive the gift of salvation, we figuratively have a new heart implanted in us. In the verses above, we see that the prophet Ezekiel foretold a covenant that God would make through Christ, and this was mentioned again in Hebrews. This is the reason why the redeemed are not just people who learn the rules. This purification of our hearts is done through the gift of salvation.

It can be difficult for us to understand that purification of our hearts is both God's responsibility and our own. How can we say it's a gift and yet have to work for it?

For though by this time you ought to be teachers, you need

> *someone to teach you again the first principles of the ora-*
> *cles of God; and you have come to need milk and not solid*
> *food. For anyone who partakes only of milk is unskilled in*
> *the word of righteousness, for he is a babe. But solid food*
> *belongs to those who are of full age, that is, those who by*
> *reason of use have their senses exercised to discern both*
> *good and evil.*
>
> **—Hebrews 5:12–14**

I like to think of this as an apprenticeship. Once we, by faith, accept the gift of salvation, we are both absolutely new to Christianity and already accepted into God's kingdom. Jesus paid the price and gave us our identity, yet we have a long way to go before we have developed the skills we need to function maturely. This is the journey of discipleship.

Think back to that wild horse. It isn't expected to know how to respond to commands or how to handle a rider immediately. Yet, if it doesn't improve over time, there's something wrong.

Similarly, God knows that we are putting to death our sinful nature and learning to develop our "say no to self" muscles. Walking closely with Him will help us to grow stronger faster, will help us to understand what He is calling us to do, and will make the sinful lifestyles we've lived in less appealing. Our hearts are growing more and more toward being pure, while all our sins are already forgiven.

Both Ezekiel and Hebrews celebrate the day when true believers can obey from pure hearts. The failure to recognize the need for a relationship rather than rules is one of the curses in churches today. Many Christians have been externally conformed to the rules instead of internally transformed by the gospel.

A Pure Heart Changes Your Desires

When You said, "Seek My face," my heart said to You, "Your face, LORD, I will seek."
> **—Psalm 27:8**

Delight yourself also in the LORD, and He shall give you the desires of your heart.
> **—Psalm 37:4**

Third, the pure heart is confirmed by a genuine change in what you want. When you develop a pure heart, it will impact your desires. The new heart will bring about new appetites. Whereas you used to long for the lust of the flesh, now you long for the purity of God. This doesn't mean you won't stumble and fall. On occasion, you may succumb to old desires. But the new heart will regain control because its driving passion is to love and please God.

A religious minded individual will obey the words of God simply because God said so. Someone with a pure heart will experience the dissipation of his or her desire for sin and will instead find pure joy in abiding in Christ.

The Evidence of Redemption

King David was called a "man after God's own heart" (Acts 13:22). Yet he sinned mightily. One of the most famous stories tells of how he had an affair with a married woman and then sent her husband to die in battle. It's pretty amazing to see David's soul-level repentance.

> *Have mercy upon me, O God, according to Your lovingkindness; according to the multitude of Your tender mercies, blot out my transgressions. Wash me thoroughly from my iniquity, and cleanse me from my sin. For I acknowledge my transgressions, and my sin is always before me.*
> **—Psalm 51:1–3**

Through this story in the Old Testament and the story of the prostitute who anointed Jesus' feet with oil in the New Testament (Luke 7:46), we can understand that God values repentance and is quick to offer forgiveness to purify our hearts and to claim us as His own.

No matter where David went or what he did, he could never get away from the fact that his heart belonged to God. His first concern after committing adultery and sin was that his "inward parts" would be cleansed (Psalm 51:6). He wanted to have the integrity of his heart restored. The Pharisees may have never sinned the way David had, but they missed the most important issue: They didn't have pure hearts before God.

Jesus favors the prostitute who comes to Him with her whole heart over the self-righteous legalist who will not give Him his heart. Christ wants the pure, unmixed, undivided, genuine, holy heart.

Such a heart is received by faith. It's implanted by the Holy Spirit. And it's confirmed by a real, noticeable change in your desires.

WORKBOOK

Chapter Seven Questions

Question: What is the state of the human heart apart from God? How is it possible to have a pure heart?

_____

_____

_____

_____

_____

_____

_____

_____

_____

_____

_____

Question: *Purification of our hearts is both God's responsibility and our own.* In what ways is God responsible to transform your heart? In what ways are you responsible?

_____

_____

_____

_____

_____

_____

_____

_____

_____

_____

_____

Action: What are your heart's desires? Write down the things you truly desire most. Do they reflect a heart that is wholly and purely set on God or a heart that is divided and idolatrous?

Journal: Meditate on Matthew 5:8 and Psalm 51. How has God sifted and cleansed your heart? Is your heart divided or whole before Christ?

Chapter Seven Notes

_____

_____

_____

_____

_____

_____

_____

_____

_____

_____

_____

_____

_____

_____

_____

_____

_____

_____

_____

_____

_____

_____

CHAPTER EIGHT

The Peacemakers

Blessed are the peacemakers, for they shall be called sons of God.

—Matthew 5:9

The essence of a peacemaker is one who accepts the sacred responsibility to diffuse grace and truth into every situation and to offer the power of the Prince of Peace.

I believe that there is something in everyone's heart that aches for peace. We all desire deep inner peace, quiet confidence, and a sense of security. A lack of this peace chips away at the human mind. Its absence wears us down. Life without peace in our homes, work, and churches is draining.

Even on a global level, we long for peace. We watch UN summits and national elections with the naïve hope that something with substance will emerge from all of the peace talks around the world. Yet time and again, treaties are trashed almost before the ink is dry on the paper.

On the news, we hear mind-numbing statistics of murder, rape, abuse, violence, and divorce, which all speak to an underlying sense of unrest. Even though history tells us that this is nothing new, we are still shocked by it.

It can be difficult to pinpoint what it is exactly that causes a lack of peace. There are so many causes. We see a lack of global peace thanks to war, natural disasters, and oppressive leaders. We see a lack of peace in the Church when there are conflicts, disagreements, and poor leadership. We see a lack of interpersonal peace when our feelings are hurt, when we are wronged by others, when we're abused, or when misunderstandings occur. We even feel a lack of inner peace when we are angry with God, refusing to forgive ourselves, or are wrestling with sin issues.

Jesus has answers for all these areas where we lack peace:

> *The Spirit of the Lord is on me, because he has anointed me to proclaim good news to the poor. He has sent me to proclaim freedom for the prisoners and recovery of sight for the blind, to set the oppressed free, to proclaim the year of the Lord's favor.*
> —**Luke 4:18–19** *(NIV)*

This Savior who is called the "Prince of Peace" (Isaiah 9:6) came into our world to answer one of the fundamental issues which every human being faces: How can we find real peace for the inner person? We've been learning that this soul rest is reserved for the broken—peace comes to those who have mourned their sin. It is embraced by people who hunger and thirst for God's righteousness.

Paul puts it this way in Romans 5:1 "Therefore, having been justified by faith, we have peace with God through our Lord Jesus Christ."

This is the peace that comes to the broken, the mourning, the gentle, the hungry, and the pure in heart. They alone can experience what it truly means to be at peace with God.

Here's an interesting thing, though, the text we are dealing with doesn't talk about those who *have* peace, but rather about the peace*makers*—those who bring peace. So, here is my question: What is a peacemaker? Let's find the answer by looking at what peacemaking is not.

Peacemaking Isn't Avoidance

There are many twisted ideas about peacemaking. When I hear the term *peacemaker* being used, the image that immediately springs to mind is that of someone who's responsible for changing the subject the moment something controversial comes up. I think of a mother distracting a whiny toddler with a toy, or a man who prefers to "go with the flow" rather than stand up to a friend making inappropriate comments. So often, the prescribed way to keep peace is to ignore the problem.

I know I'm not the only one who pictures this. You have more than likely seen this scenario: You're at a big family holiday meal. Everyone knows that Aunt Sue and Cousin Mark had a big blowup that is still unresolved, so everyone tiptoes around it. Rather than encouraging them to clear the air, we carefully hide it behind formality and call it "keeping the peace." We avoid confrontation at all cost.

There is a phrase I heard one time called a "no-talk rule." These are certain issues that, thorough an unspoken understanding, we realize must not be spoken of at home, work, or in the Church. We can't talk about them because there are differing opinions that can't coexist. And this "no-talk rule" is applied to create a kind of unspoken neutrality that we wrongly call peace.

If controversy is avoided at all cost, nobody gets upset, angry, or hurt. At best, this is little more than a short-lived ceasefire. No one deals with the real issues when they embrace this kind of behavior in the name of peace. This is a perverted parody of peacemaking. It is a pretend peace. Christ clearly taught there are two types of peace.

> Peace I leave with you, My peace I give to you; not as the world gives do I give to you. Let not your heart be troubled, neither let it be afraid.
> —*John 14:27*

Worldly peace can simply mean there is an absence of conflict. This is not true peace. We can get people to put down their guns and stop shooting for a few days, but it doesn't change their rage and hatred toward one another. Society tries to put an end to yelling but does nothing about deep resentments. Even the Church at times chooses to handle conflict by avoiding issues and pretending everything is fine.

This is not the peace that Christ gives. It is the worldly,

external, counterfeit version of peace better known as avoidance. Jesus wants to go to the heart and deal with the real issues. Anything that fails to get to the truth and resolve the problem is not peace.

Peacemaking Tells the Truth in Love

Over the years as a church leader, I have heard many stories of abuse, pain, and sorrow that people have experienced at the hands of others. Many of these stories take a sad turn when the hurting people confide in a trusted person but are then told to stay quiet. For fear of rocking the boat and upsetting the sense of peace, people choose to punish the victims rather than the perpetrators. They think if they just keep the assault or sin hidden that it will keep the peace.

Many of these victims spend years in self-loathing and self-blame for something that is not their fault. It's as if they can never get full healing and deliverance because it was not validated by the trusted person to whom they chose to finally expose their deepest hurts.

Hurt feelings don't occur because a big bully is out to stomp on me. Hurt feelings are a naturally occurring part of every relationship. If we spend our lives trying to avoid hurting feelings, or if we are looking to have our hurt feelings petted or even worshiped, we aren't living in the fullness of God's grace.

Sometimes being a peacemaker means understanding another person's motivation and choosing whether or not to go to the person to lovingly discuss the hurt. If I've had a bad day at work and my wife says something to me, it might bruise my feelings. Yet I know that it wasn't her intention and that I was being overly sensitive. Running to her to demand an apology isn't beneficial in that particular situation.

If I have a co-worker who regularly comes to my office and points out everything she doesn't like that I'm doing, it might be a different story. Setting boundaries is okay. I need to remember that my co-worker isn't trying to be hurtful and probably doesn't realize that I don't like her criticisms. But talking with her kindly might be the best way to make peace.

Blessed are the peacemakers who wisely consider what truth needs to be told and who then do so with love. Blessed are those who encourage the hurting to find the strength to open themselves up and find healing.

Confronting things on the way to real peace is usually not easy. In extreme cases, it could even have serious consequences. God wants peace in the world, our homes, and the Church. But the peace He brings and the peace He calls us to is not born of silence, avoidance, ego, and politics.

Peace Through Purity and Truth

> *But the wisdom that comes from heaven is first of all pure; then peace-loving, considerate, submissive, full of mercy and good fruit, impartial and sincere. Peacemakers who sow in peace raise a harvest of righteousness.*
> *—James 3:17–18 (NIV)*

God's wisdom is, first of all, marked by truth. Second,

it is peace loving. Any form of peace that isn't rooted in truth is false. We will never get peace by pretending everything is okay when it's not. Wisdom from God finds its way to peace through purity and truth. It confronts what is real and exposes what is false.

Peacemakers are exactly the opposite of what I previously assumed. They do not appease and avoid conflict at all cost. Rather, they move into it with courage to resist, confront, disagree, and obey God in order to achieve real peace.

Jesus often called the Pharisees hypocrites (Matthew 15:7; Matthew 22:18; Matthew 23:13). Why did He make such a harsh statement if He wanted peace? Because Jesus knew that real peace can't happen without honesty. It isn't based on feeling good, being popular, or never stepping on toes. It is born of loving truthfulness.

Did Jesus love the Pharisees? Yes, He loved them deeply. Jesus loved the Pharisees and knew what was in their souls, because He was God. While His words seem harsh to us, Jesus knew what the Pharisees needed to hear and He didn't shy away from uncovering the truth.

When we are willing to confront problems like that, it changes the location of the conflict. It moves it from inside the heart and puts it outside in the open. When we ignore the problem, we have fake peace outside and a raging war on the inside.

Before I move on to the next section, here is a warning for you. What has been taught so far has the potential to stir up a lot of carnal confrontations. Real peacemakers will confront truth and break "no-talk" rules. But understand this: The ultimate goal of genuine peacemakers is healing, not hurting. It is possible to go too far the other way. Telling everyone exactly what you think of them because it's "the truth" can be just as damaging. It is possible to misuse truth as a sledgehammer to hurt and humiliate people. If we challenge people just to win an argument, we are not involved in Kingdom work. Our strategy must be like Jesus'—bringing real peace through the truth in order to restore.

In the same way that we can pervert the true meaning of peacemaking, it is also possible to subvert peace. Even the most well-meaning peacemaker can come up against some challenges that will prevent peace from growing.

General Sin

First, sin is an enemy to peace. Each of us has a sinful nature that seeks to undo peace at every turn. The sins of pride and fear can keep us from hearing what someone has to say when we are confronted. Superiority can twist our desires to find peace into a show where we want to win the "Best Christian" prize and taint our words and attitudes. The desire to be the one "in the know" can tempt us to gossip about other people as they strive to work through a disagreement toward peace.

The enemy can turn anything that is good into something sinful. Abiding with God is the only way to keep checking our attitudes against His best plan and not let sin get a foothold in our attempts for peace.

Inability to Receive

Second, the inability to receive the fullness of our redemption is an enemy of peace. We can know that we are forgiven without really letting that truth in our hearts. For many reasons, we find it difficult to accept grace, love, and forgiveness. When we can't accept these things, it's harder for us to extend them to others.

Jesus said, "My yoke is easy and My burden is light" (Matthew 11:30). He didn't say there was no yoke and no burden. Rather, the yoke is grace and the burden is having faith to receive the grace. Sometimes we are called to difficult things, but the grace we are offered through faith will make the difficult things bearable.

Circumstances

Third, external circumstances can become an enemy to our peace. We sometimes make our experience of God's peace dependent on other things. We look to our kids, our jobs, our spouses, or material things for peace for our souls. We say things like, "If only I had a better job, if only my kids were ___ , if only my husband were more ___ , then I would have peace."

If this is true, then all of these issues must line up just right in order to have peace. You can guess just exactly how often that happens! Besides, temporary peace is like dust in our mouths, because it never lasts and it never satisfies our spiritual thirst.

The Call

> Popularity has slain more prophets of God than persecution ever did.[12]
> —**Vance Havner**

In Isaiah 9:6, against a backdrop of Old Testament prophecy, Scripture declares Jesus to be the prince of peace. Yet it seems that most places He went ended up experiencing a lack of earthly peace. The Hebrew phrase for "prince of peace" in Isaiah 9:6 is *sar shalom*. This (*sar*) is such an interesting choice of word because it has militaristic overtones. It literally refers to a royal commander or warlord.[13]

We cannot take any of the beatitudes at face value, but must understand them as Christ intended. With this in mind, it's essential we realize that Jesus did not come to make *earthly* peace but to establish the peace of God.

Yes, He was a peacemaker and calls us to be the same. But more specifically, Jesus is the warlord of peace, whose birth was announced, fittingly, by "a multitude of the heavenly host" (Luke 2:13)—"host" being the Greek word for a militia. It is a Greek idiom, meaning "heavenly army."[14] Jesus is the military commander of heaven who, instead of waging war against us, came to die for us to secure our peace.

This is what makes the angel's announcement of Jesus' birth in Luke 2:11–14 especially intriguing—because it proclaims the fulfillment of the promise from Isaiah 9:6

in the birth of Christ. Jesus arrived to command the heavenly campaign to destroy the chaos that opposes peace. He came to make peace. Therefore, Jesus is the true peacemaker.

Peacemakers can quickly become peacekeepers (or appeasers) if they allow fear to guide them, rather than love. If you are a peacemaker, be prepared for what will come with that. There will be times and seasons of great Kingdom fruit, but there will also be persecution and disdain from the world.

You will be identified as a child of God when you are a peacemaker. Let that sink in for a minute. Blessed are those who bring the ministry of peace, healing, forgiveness, grace, and reconciliation to a lost and dying world. Peacemakers will bring light to where darkness once was. They will speak truth where lies once lived. They will bring reality and holiness where hypocrisy once ruled. They will deliver grace where legalism was the rule. These are the things that Jesus did.

When we are peacemakers, we are counted as God's children. What a heavy responsibility—and what an incredible privilege!

WORKBOOK

Chapter Eight Questions

Question: What is the difference between being a peace-maker and a peacekeeper? How does speaking the truth in love relate to peacemaking?

_____

_____

_____

_____

_____

_____

_____

_____

_____

_____

_____

Question: When is it hard for you to confront a problem? When is it hard for you to be gentle in your approach? How can you be a peacemaker for someone who needs to unburden their heart about a wrong done to them?

_____

_____

_____

_____

_____

_____

_____

_____

_____

_____

_____

Action: Study the book of Philemon and Paul's Spirit-led peacemaking between a wronged master and a runaway slave. What practical peacemaking tips can you learn from this short book?

Journal: Meditate on Matthew 5:9 and James 3:17–18. How are you diffusing grace and truth into the various realms of your life (marriage, parenting, ministry, employment, community, etc.)?

Chapter Eight Notes

_____

_____

_____

_____

_____

_____

_____

_____

_____

_____

_____

_____

_____

_____

_____

_____

_____

_____

_____

_____

_____

_____

CHAPTER NINE

The Persecuted

*Blessed are those who are persecuted for righteousness'
sake, for theirs is the kingdom of heaven.*

*Blessed are you when they revile and persecute you, and
say all kinds of evil against you falsely for My sake. Rejoice
and be exceedingly glad, for great is your reward in
heaven, for so they persecuted the prophets who were before you.*

—Matthew 5:10–12

What picture comes to mind when you hear the phrase
"religious persecution"? Do you imagine the Roman col-
iseum under the reign of Nero? Do you think of the
underground Church in closed countries? What about here
in the United States? Do believe you face any religious
persecution here?

*The essence of the persecution arises when the Spirit
of God in you is at war with the spirit of the world in others.*

Christian persecution encompasses any hostility experienced from the world as a result of one's identification as a Christian. From verbal harassment to hostile feelings, attitudes, and actions, Christians in parts of the world with severe religious restrictions pay a heavy price for their faith. Beatings, physical torture, confinement, isolation, severe punishment, imprisonment, slavery, discrimination in education and employment, and even death are just a few examples of the persecution they experience on a daily basis.

When I read the Bible and consider Church history, I see many stories of people who were persecuted and reviled simply for their faith. I remember how Christ was reviled and crucified for the simple gospel message. I think of how many of the apostles were martyred for spreading the gospel. As I began to look at this Beatitude and compare it to what I read in the Bible, it seemed somewhat far off, something of the past.

I live in the United States of America. We have religious freedoms that typically keep us sheltered from persecution. It seems like persecution for faith, at least in this country, may be a thing of the past. However, the longer I live, the more I see the climate of our world and country drastically changing in this area. I also have come to understand that persecution comes in all shapes, forms, and sizes, and that true Kingdom children will likely experience some form of persecution for righteousness' sake at some point in their lives.

As I write this book, the latest statistics show that Christians are the most persecuted people group on a global scale. Each month 322 Christians are killed for their faith. Each month 214 churches and Christian properties are destroyed. Each month 772 forms of violence are committed against Christians—atrocities like beatings, abductions, rapes, arrests, and forced marriages.[15]

According to the Pew Research Center, over 75 percent of the world's population lives in areas with severe religious restrictions. Christians in more than sixty countries face persecution from their governments or surrounding neighbors simply because of their belief in Jesus Christ.[16]

Persecution Personalized

Sometimes it's hard to know how to feel about persecution. Jesus said we are blessed for it, yet persecution doesn't appear in North America in the same ways it does in other countries. At the same time, no one looks at someone who's been jailed for his faith and thinks, "Oh, I wish I could be persecuted like that!" I've heard many Christians pray and thank God that there isn't persecution in our country at this point in time.

Is that wrong? Well, yes and no. We do understand that there is blessing in persecution. Those who stand up for their faith and take insults, or even physical punishment, experience God in a way that the rest of us rarely do. When we abandon our comfort for the gospel's sake and are persecuted for it, we follow in Jesus' own footsteps. And, quite honestly, the Church doesn't grow as greatly in strength or in numbers as it does in countries where persecution doesn't happen.

But let's also not forget that there are other, less dramatic, kinds of persecution that Christians even in the most "tolerant" countries face. We do not want to start comparing whose suffering is worse or which group experiences more persecution. Don't feel bad if you live in a place with less persecution. However, we should be mindful of our brothers and sisters in chains and use our religious freedoms to advance the gospel.

Persecution Is Real

Yes, and all who desire to live godly in Christ Jesus will suffer persecution.
                                              —2 Timothy 3:12

Persecution is a reality of Kingdom life, and it is evidence that we are a part of it. It's common for Christians to look for proof of our conversion, and God supplies evidence of peace, joy, and love. However, one piece of evidence we don't look for is conflict and persecution. The spirit that is in you is in direct opposition to what is in the world.

If we take this one step further, we must acknowledge that if we never see opposition or persecution on some level, we might not be living our lives in the way that God calls us to live. We all know sin exists, we all see it around us, and we are all expected to do something about it. Living a life that is free from conflict might indicate that we are compromising.

We can tell many things about believers by who opposes them. Who is on our side and who is against us? If we're not creating some kind of stir as individual believers or as a body in our community, we can rest assured that we are not advancing the Kingdom in a way that we should.

Let's take a look at how Paul saw himself in the ministry:

> For I think that God has displayed us, the apostles, last, as men condemned to death; for we have been made a spectacle to the world, both to angels and to men.
> **—1 Corinthians 4:9**

The phrase "condemned to die" is a direct reference to parades that took place in Corinth. As the Romans would march triumphantly through town, they would display the spoils of war. At the back of the line was a group of people who had been captured in battle. These prisoners were stripped, bound, and sentenced to die. After the parade, the crowds would file into the arena to watch these people get eaten alive by animals or burned at the stake.

Paul's perception was that when he gave his life to Christ, he laid his life on the line. He signed up for a trip to the arena. In the words of Dietrich Bonhoeffer in *The Cost of Discipleship*, "When Jesus bids a man to come, He bids him to come to die."[17] There will always be opposition and persecution for those who follow Christ.

Contrast that with the all-too-common evangelistic ministries that promise comfort and prosperity "if you just believe and send your contribution." We parade celebrities, athletes, and entertainers before non-believers so they can rest assured that it is cool to be a Christian.

The hard truth is, if you're a peacemaker and a truth

bearer who confronts sin, then you will be opposed—guaranteed.

The Root of Persecution

Where will this opposition come from? Persecution will come from the world, but let's divide that into two parts.

First, the opposition will come from the world that is in the Church. This is a powerful tactic of Satan. If he can render the Church impotent by keeping us content in carnality, the Kingdom of God will never get to the world.

> *Behold, I send you out as sheep in the midst of wolves. Therefore, be wise as serpents and harmless as doves. But beware of men, for they will deliver you up to councils and scourge you in their synagogues. You will be brought before governors and kings for My sake, as a testimony to them and to the Gentiles. But when they deliver you up, do not worry about how or what you should speak. For it will be given to you in that hour what you should speak; for it is not you who speak, but the Spirit of your Father who speaks in you.*
>
> *Now brother will deliver up brother to death, and a father his child; and children will rise up against parents and cause them to be put to death. And you will be hated by all for My name's sake. But he who endures to the end will be saved.*
> **—Matthew 10:16–22**

The first wave of opposition for the disciples was going to be from the Pharisees, scribes, and the chief priests. These first members of the "wolf pack" were the ones who "attended church" faithfully and observed the Law. This demonstrates the fact that there is "the world within the church" (those with no heart change) and "the church in the church" (those who are internally changed).

I know all of this may sound harsh, but I can't deny what Scripture says over and over again.

Many times, the persecution from the outside is much easier to spot, deal with, and move past. The persecution from within is very difficult to eradicate—that which comes from those with whom you have relationship and fellowship. These are people that you have done life with, and the relational breakdown may be much more difficult to handle and deal with.

Take Adam, for example. His wife cheated on him, and their breakup turned nasty on both parts. The resulting divorce devastated him and, after the dust had settled, Adam found himself taking a hard look at the man he'd become. He realized he needed God and began to attend church.

Over the next weeks, Adam found the hope and forgiveness he'd been needing. He grew excited about following Christ and asked his pastor if he could start a ministry for divorced men through the church.

The pastor was quick to say yes, and Adam started off with enthusiasm. Yet, he was stunned to begin to feel backlash from other members of the congregation. At a members' meeting, someone stood up and said that the Bible said it was wrong to get a divorce. Having a group for divorced men made it sound like this church approved of divorce, and this wasn't something they should be a part of.

In no time, the church was dividing into those for the

group and those opposed. Adam decided to do what was right and went to the church member who had first expressed concern. Hoping to smooth things over, Adam explained what it had been like as he came to Christ following his divorce and how he hoped to do the same for others.

Unfortunately, this woman took offense and refused to back down. She started to discuss Adam at length with anyone who would listen. Before long, Adam began to dislike attending church events. He felt the disapproval of the people around him and struggled to hold firm to the knowledge that his group for divorced men was making a difference for the Kingdom of God.

Second, opposition will come from the outside world. When the Church is following the Lord's leading and actively partnering with Him in His work, we then face the opposition of the world itself. This army has Satan himself as commander in chief.

> God assumed from the beginning that the wise of the world would view Christians as fools ... and He has not been disappointed.... If I have brought any message today, it is this: Have the courage to have your wisdom regarded as stupidity. Be fools for Christ. And have the courage to suffer the contempt of the sophisticated world.[18]
>
> **—Antonin Scalia, Supreme Court Justice**

I am not yet convinced that the American evangelical world has advanced past the first wave of opposition. But when we bring the Kingdom powerfully to the world, it will not be welcomed by many. The good news is this:

The Kingdom of God will be embraced by some who will be born again by the Spirit, and the persecution will not thwart what God will do to make His name famous and draw many unto Him.

Response to Persecution

This sounds a bit crazy to me, but remember that these Beatitudes are Kingdom principles that sound backward in view of our cultural norms. Jesus tells us that we are blessed when we are reviled and persecuted. He tells us to rejoice—that is, to be filled to overflowing with joy and gladness. Wow! How contrary is that to our human, fleshly responses?

There are several reasons to rejoice when we are persecuted:

First, we can rejoice because the Kingdom is ours. This is a future promise for joy in heaven, a promise for an eternity that has yet to come true. This is also a present-day promise for now. So, in the context of our suffering, in the midst of being reviled for peacemaking and focusing on what matters, we can feel and experience the Kingdom of God and His power.

It is clear in the lives of the early Church that the people had a joy that was not from their circumstances or situation (Philippians 4:10–13). This joy was directly from God, and it gave them the grace needed for what they were enduring. They were walking in the Kingdom of God, and that experience was greater than the persecution to which they were being exposed.

Daniel illustrates this truth in a vivid way (Daniel 6).

He was thrown into a lions' den because of an unyielding obedience to God. Daniel brought brokenness and mourning and God's kingdom to His culture. As a result of that, he sat only a few inches away from razor-sharp lions' teeth that could kill him in seconds. He was undoubtedly scared. Wouldn't you be? Even though he had faith God would save him, I am sure it was not an easy night. But because of persecution and his obedience to God, the Lord delivered him, and He was magnified. Daniel experienced the Kingdom in that moment.

You may be thinking, What about the ones who don't get delivered? Where is the glory in that?

Consider Stephen in Acts 7:54–60. He was sentenced to be stoned to death for preaching the gospel. Would you say he experienced the Kingdom in that moment, or the Kingdom of the future? Consider one detail in this story. We know that Jesus is "sitting" at the right hand of the Father because He has finished the work of redemption (Romans 8:34). But in this story, we are told that Stephen saw Christ "standing at the right hand of God" (Acts 7:56). What does this mean? Even while Stephen was dying, Jesus was right there giving him the power of the Kingdom—even to die. That is both Kingdom now and Kingdom future.

Second, we can rejoice because we receive a great reward. Our life here on earth is brief in comparison to eternity, but what we do here matters in the long-term scale of forever. A little suffering here cannot compare to what awaits us.

Therefore we do not lose heart. Even though our outward

man is perishing, yet the inward man is being renewed day by day. For our light affliction, which is but for a moment, is working for us a far more exceeding and eternal weight of glory, while we do not look at the things which are seen, but at the things which are not seen. For the things, which are seen are temporary, but the things which are not seen are eternal.

—2 Corinthians 4:16–18

When you obey God and live your life for His purposes, it produces an eternal reward that supersedes any pain, persecution, or suffering you may endure in this life.

The Bible talks about crowns we will wear (Revelation 4:10; Psalm 103:4; Psalm 149:4). I don't imagine these are actual crowns. Why would we even want one in heaven? I am not fully sure what they are, but if God gives them, you know that they are good.

This, too, is a present reality. We enjoy part of this reward now as we worship and adore our Savior and exhibit the glory of God in our daily lives. The Holy Spirit, His gifts, fruits, and manifestation in your life is a reward and an aspect of the gift of salvation.

Third, we can rejoice in persecution because we are in good company. If we are being reviled, opposed, and persecuted because of our brokenness and for the sake of righteousness, here is some very good news: We will be mentioned in the same breath with Isaiah, Jeremiah, Daniel, Hosea, Paul, Peter, and Jesus, just to name a few. We are fighting the right fight if we are in this fight. Rejoice. Be glad. We are in good company.

Then Jesus said to His disciples, "If anyone desires to come

> *after Me, let him deny himself, and take up his cross, and follow Me. For whoever desires to save his life will lose it, but whoever loses his life for My sake will find it. For what profit is it to a man if he gains the whole world, and loses his own soul? Or what will a man give in exchange for his soul?"*
>
> **—Matthew 16:24–26**

When you find true brokenness and start down this journey of discipleship in Christ, you lay down your life before Him. Your life is no longer your own. Living in the Beatitudes will cost you everything. The call to discipleship is a call to die. When you understand this, you realize that, although persecution is hard spiritually, emotionally, and physically, you already counted the cost and have the gift of grace needed to live this out. When persecution arises, do not become disillusioned because you know whose you are, and you know that He has your life in His hand (Job 12:10).

Persecution Is a Catalyst for Church Growth

My personal view on persecution for righteousness' sake has changed drastically over the years.

As I have journeyed as a disciple of Christ, I have seen that my life clearly is not my own. I have laid a lot of things down at the Lord's feet, leading me to be where I am with Him. This is nothing more than allowing Him to be Lord of my life. It is nothing special or unique when you look at biblical characteristics of a disciple of Christ.

Over the past five years, I have done a lot of prayerful

reflection and study on this topic. I thank God for the nation I live in and appreciate all the liberties and rights afforded to me. However, I have come to see that religious freedom can be an amazing tool to spread the gospel, or it can be the very recipe for apathetic, lazy Christianity. Religious freedom has the ability to create a moral society that has little desire for relationship with God.

Many of us have been baptized into a nationalistic, American idea of Christianity (a kind of cultural Christianity), rather than Christ. We assume to be American is to be a Christian. Many of us have fallen for a subculture of true Christianity that is a westernized counterfeit of the truth.

I firmly believe that trials and persecution will expose what is in your heart and clearly show you where you are on this discipleship journey. Trials and persecution will produce or affirm brokenness, or they will reveal carnality.

I have spent some time over the past few years with some leaders within the persecuted Church on a global scale. What is amazing to me is how they view the persecution and their relative lack of religious freedom. They see God work miraculously in their midst, often through persecution, in ways that we don't commonly see in countries that have laws protecting religion.

I heard one of these leaders talking about how we can pray for them specifically. He said, "Don't pray for us— pray with us as if you are in chains with us. Don't pray for our deliverance from this persecution, but rather pray that God use this as an open door to show His glory." Wow! What a different perspective from the perspective that most of us have.

> ...and for me, that utterance may be given to me, that I may open my mouth boldly to make known the mystery of the gospel, for which I am an ambassador in chains; that in it I may speak boldly, as I ought to speak.
> —*Ephesians 6:19–20*

Paul asked that they pray for him that, in his persecution, he may be bold for the gospel's sake. Moments of tension become open doors for the Church to bring the Kingdom of God to the earth. I ask, are we allowing God to lead us down these paths, or are we praying for Him to remove them from us? Are we using the persecution we experience to deepen our faith and bring gospel context? Are we experiencing persecution for righteousness' sake at all?

Persecution will be a natural repercussion of becoming more like Christ as you abide in Him. However, it is this abiding relationship which will give you the boldness and courage to continue walking full of faith in the face of persecution.

Chapter Nine Questions

Question: How would you define persecution for Christ's sake? Have you ever experienced persecution? What was your response?

_____

_____

_____

_____

_____

_____

_____

_____

_____

_____

_____

Question: What is the difference between how the American church views persecution and how the underground church views it? What are the hidden blessings of persecution? What should be the blessings of religious freedom?

_____

_____

_____

_____

_____

_____

_____

_____

_____

_____

_____

_____

Action: Become informed and involved in helping or praying for the persecuted church through a ministry such as OpenDoors or Voice of the Martyrs.

Journal: Mediate on Matthew 5:10–12 and Matthew 16:24–26. How is the Holy Spirit within you different from the spirit of the world around you?

Chapter Nine Notes

_____

_____

_____

_____

_____

_____

_____

_____

_____

_____

_____

_____

_____

_____

_____

_____

_____

_____

_____

_____

_____

_____

CONCLUSION

Response to the Beatitudes

I want to say thank you for investing your time in the reading of this book. I pray that God has used this to open your heart to deeper revelation and experience in Him. There is a lot to be learned in these lessons, but the principles are lifelong and transformative.

The Beatitudes point the way into that intimate place with a pure and holy God. Religion keeps you on the outside, but these axioms with which Jesus began His ministry are drawing you into the heart of the Father. Isn't it amazing when you really look at the heart of the Beatitudes that they are a combination of who you are, what you do, and what happens to you? Taken all together, the Beatitudes encompass the fullness of your life.

Like I have said throughout this book, abiding closely with God is a process. Walking through the Beatitudes in this way has the potential to change your life for His glory. It is a powerful foundation that Jesus laid at the beginning of the Sermon on the Mount. Everything else He taught seems to flow from these foundational teachings. At the end of His sermon we read the following:

> *And so it was, when Jesus had ended these sayings, that the people were astonished at His teaching, for He taught them as one having authority, and not as the scribes.*
> **—Matthew 7:28–29**

What was so different about Jesus that astonished the crowds? It was that He had authority that the scribes did not have. The scribes had the authority to copy the written words of the Torah, oral traditions, and other Jewish writings in that day. That seems like authority to me. Why was it different with Jesus?

The scribes had the written word and religion. Jesus was empowered by the Holy Spirit. The Holy Spirit is a key ingredient to authority. When you are abiding in Christ, the Holy Spirit is given to you, and you are empowered to live with authority, power, grace, spiritual gifts, and fruit. Walking through the Beatitudes is a way to tap in to that authority in your personal life.

The same unspoken question Christ put to them is now put to you. What will your response to His message be?

In the text above, we see that the crowds heard all of this and were left with astonishment. These crowds were hearing things they had perhaps never heard before. Or perhaps they were hearing things they had heard before, but this time it came from someone with firsthand knowledge and authority and rather than through interpretation.

The Word of God is living and active. You can learn

the Word, be astonished by the Word, and yet choose not to allow it to change your life. Just hearing is not going to produce lasting fruit in your life. Abiding with Jesus means living a life of faith in obedience to His Word.

> But be doers of the word, and not hearers only, deceiving yourselves. For if anyone is a hearer of the word and not a doer, he is like a man observing his natural face in a mirror; for he observes himself, goes away, and immediately forgets what kind of man he was. But he who looks into the perfect law of liberty and continues in it, and is not a forgetful hearer but a doer of the work, this one will be blessed in what he does.
> —James 1:22–25

You have the choice to either believe or reject God's Word. If you choose to act on the words of God in faith, it will produce a harvest in your life. If you choose to be a hearer only, you miss the true purpose and blessing, and you will not reap the benefits that come from obeying God's Word. What type of hearer are you going to be?

Abide in Christ

In my many years of ministry in the context of American church culture, I hear a lot of people who are sincerely seeking truth about how to follow Christ. My simple response to so many is, "Shut up and abide." Silence the other voices in your life; only allow the voice of the Bible and the Holy Spirit to direct you. Remain in Him, and don't let any voice, including your own, remove you from that sacred place.

There are many things to which you may not know the answers—some you may never know. There are many topics within the church world on which you differ from others. Instead of getting caught up in dissension, arguments, and discord, learn to stand in your identity in Christ. If He wants you to have revelation or learning in those areas, He will direct your path there.

When you abide in Christ, quick answers to your questions are no longer satisfying. You learn to become intimate with Christ, and He guides and directs your steps and satisfies your heart's desires. Many of the complicated topics are made clear through understanding and spiritual growth as you abide in Christ. In some cases, your questions may not receive an answer this side of heaven—instead they may require you to walk in faith, trusting God to be true to His Word.

This progression of living into the Beatitudes opens wide the doorway to an intimate abiding relationship with Christ. As we truly embrace each of the Beatitudes, we will unlock the secrets of abiding in the Lord, and we will never be the same. Discipleship is not about arriving, but about abiding in Christ.

Then, Jesus said to those Jews who believed Him, "If you abide in My word, you are My disciples indeed."
—John 8:31

The model that Christ gave us for following Him is so simple that it confounds the wise of this world (1 Corinthians 1:27 KJV). Jesus told us to simply remain connected to Him. That's it. No ten-step programs or charts of accomplishment. Just stay connected to Him. Abide in Him.

As we have laid out in this book, God loves you with an everlasting love. He wants to intimately know you, and have you know Him, before He ever wants you to do anything for Him. He wants to be loved by you without condition. All of this only happens in an abiding relationship. The verse above tells us that, apart from Him, we can do nothing that lasts. We need Him so desperately.

Remove Jesus from Your To-Do List

Jesus does not want you to put Him at the top of your list of things to do for the day. Many Christians view their relationship with Him this way. They check off spending time with Him like they would a grocery list or a list of household chores, but Jesus wants to be the center of your life. He wants everything else in your life to flow through your relationship with Him. This is totally different than being an item on your list.

Outside of abiding in Christ, you will have an uncultivated soul, overgrown with briars, thorns, and thistles. At the end of your life, you will look back and realize you did a lot of things for God. You had good days and bad. You had victories and failures. You obeyed His Word and sinned against Him. All of this should be swallowed up in a loving relationship with Him. If you're banking on anything else, then you will be greatly disappointed. If you remained in Him, then you will have produced fruit. You will have allowed Him to prune you so that you could grow. You will have done something that mattered because it was centered on Christ.

Where do you start on this relationship? What do you do first?

I have pointed you to the Beatitudes. These foundational ideas sum up so much about what it means to be a follower of Christ. No wonder Jesus began His Sermon on the Mount with them!

Begin by asking God to help you grow in these areas. As you read the Bible, note how often the things that the writers are saying come directly back to the Beatitudes. It might take a lifetime to get a handle on all of these, but as you abide in Jesus, you will continually draw closer to demonstrating them all.

Conclusion Questions

Question: What was different about the way Jesus taught versus the teachings of the Pharisees and scribes? How can a follower of Jesus also have spiritual authority?

_____

_____

_____

_____

_____

_____

_____

_____

_____

_____

_____

Question: What is the difference between doing Christian things and abiding in Christ? Which one characterizes your life? How can the same action (e.g., reading the Bible) be a religious ritual or the fruit of an abiding relationship?

_____

_____

_____

_____

_____

_____

_____

_____

_____

_____

Action: If you have not done so already, commit the Beatitudes to memory. Incorporate them into your prayer and devotional life. Ask an accountability partner to help keep you responsible to grow in these areas. Remember, they are not a to-do list, but the outflow of an abiding relationship with God.

Journal: Meditate on James 1:22–25 and how you will apply the truths of this book to your daily life.

Conclusion Notes

APPENDIX A

Journaling 101

The following information on journaling is used with permission from Rocky Fleming at www.Influencers.org.[19]

On your journey to intimacy with Christ, one thing that can greatly assist you is journaling. This is a foreign concept to most people. However, journaling can be a gift from God to you. Many times, we learn to internalize our thoughts, keeping them hidden in the deep recesses of our minds. Journaling is a way to help you get those issues out of your heart and onto the altar before God.

In this technological age of high-speed communication, written words have been lost. Today, most of our thoughts and reflections about life—if they even make it out of our heads—are condensed into brief digital formats, which are then deleted in cyberspace before they have a chance to sink into our consciousness. There is power in the written word on paper. God wants us to slow down, be still for a few moments with Him, and just like He instructed countless people from Moses to Paul, He wants us to write down the revelations He gives us.

In the pages of this book, there is a lot of information for you to prayerfully navigate. We have included this simple form of journaling to help you put down on paper some key things that may be speaking the loudest to you. When you write things down there is a tendency to remember more and create further action steps to implement the learning pieces. If you are going to invest the time to read this book, it would greatly benefit you to utilize journaling through the workbook section at the end of each chapter. If you are inspired to become an abiding leader of an abiding church, there will be much to process, and this method can help you to simplify this.

STAR Journaling Exercise Template

#1 Scripture Read/Promise Given/Question Asked

Read the verse and/or question and walk through the STAR/SPAR process. Pause and prayerfully meditate on what is being said, read, or asked.

#2 Thought Conveyed/Promise Given

In this part, write down what this means to you so that you can clearly understand the question, scripture, thought, or promise. Make it personal to get the most out of it.

#3 Application Made

How does this teaching apply to me right now? How does this apply to my leadership context?

#4 Response Given

What can I do to immediately to apply this to my life? How should I respond/react to this promise or instruction? What are some long-term things I need to respond to?

APPENDIX B

Further Resources

The Journey is a nine- to twelve-month process, with most groups meeting every other week. It is divided into three main segments, called Enlightened, Enabled, and Expressing.

The Enlightened segment of the Journey is the foundation of the process. The step-by-step understanding of the four personal aspects of God (He Knows, He Cares, He Is Willing, and He Is Able) is designed to help the participant realize that God is a loving, caring, and intimate God who wants to involve Himself in every area of the participant's life. This new understanding should guide the participant to the goal of being willing to trust God with his life and prepares the way for the second segment of the Journey.

The Enabled segment of the Journey focuses on an abiding, intimate relationship with Jesus. This segment helps the participant understand how the Holy Spirit "enables" him to develop this new level of intimacy. He is guided through an understanding of the "fruit of the

Spirit" and how this fruit enables the use of the "gifts of the Spirit." This should help him to better understand his role and purpose in the work of God's kingdom. Above all else, the Enabled segment should guide the participant toward the goal of releasing control of his life and experiencing the joy of personal abandonment found in his abiding relationship with Jesus.

The Expressing segment of the Journey is the culmination of the Journey process. The principles of "Being a God Seeker," "Being a God Abider," and "Live It Out" are used as the guide to help the participant fully understand the entire Journey. He is introduced to the concept of servant leadership within his marriage, his family, and the world around him. He is challenged to grasp the concept of "blooming where he is planted" and how he is now ready to partner with God to influence his world in a supernatural way. At the end of the Journey, the participant is released to take the name "Influencer" and begin to bear fruit that lasts by expressing Christlike love to all those around him.

The Journey experience has three main components for each participant.

The first is his personal "treasure hunt," conducted during the days between sessions. This is the core of the Journey and the place where heart transformation takes place. This "treasure hunt" guides the participant toward the "Inner Chamber," where intimacy with Christ is discovered and experienced.

The second component is the one-on-one time between the guide and the participant. This individual time is critical to the participant's journey as the guide and the participant share their life stories.

The third component is the group sessions, designed for the group to discuss their journey and share discovered truth. Each session enhances the other two components and ties the Journey together.

This Journey process will lay a strong foundation that you can build upon as you pursue your long-term growth track.

Influencers is a ministry with the goal of guiding people into an intimate, abiding relationship with Jesus Christ. They accomplish this through Journey groups, who journey together for nine months, each desiring a closer proximity to the Father. Participants discover God in a most personal way through Scripture, journaling, group discussion, prayer, and study materials.

Jesus said, "I am the vine; you are the branches. If you remain in me and I in you, you will bear much fruit; apart from me you can do nothing" (John 15:5 NIV). For years, good Christian people have been striving to bear fruit for God. However, they have missed the part about "remaining in Him." Influencers helps people press the pause button in life, so that they can take time to seek Jesus and find renewed hope and purpose.

Thousands of people—and increasingly, women and married couples as well—have gone on this Journey worldwide, and thousands more are finding their way to this life-giving process. If you would like to know more about Influencers and the Journey and how to start a group in your city, go to the website at www.influencers.org.

Other Resources

- *I'm a Catalyst* membership manual by Catalyst Church
- *Abiding Church: Creating, Cultivating, and Stewarding a Culture of Discipleship* by Nate Sweeney
- *Abiding in Identity: Who I Am Because of Whose I Am* by Nate Sweeney
- *Journey to the Inner Chamber* by Rocky Fleming
- *Knowing Christ and Making Him Known* by Nate Sweeney
- *5-2-1 Leadership Planning*

REFERENCES

Notes

1. "Beatitude." *Oxford English Living Dictionaries.* Oxford University Press. https://en.oxforddictionaries.com/definition/beatitude.
2. MacArthur, John. *The MacArthur New Testament Commentary.* Moody, 2011.
3. Fleming, Rocky, "Journaling." *Influencers Global Ministries.* www.influencers.org/journaling.
4. *ESV Study Bible.* Kindle edition. Crossway, 2008.
5. *ESV Study Bible.*
6. "Strong's G4434 – ptōchos." *Blue Letter Bible.* https://www.blueletterbible.org/lang/lexicon/lexicon.cfm?Strongs=G4434&t=KJV.
7. "Strong's G3997 – penthos." *Blue Letter Bible.* https://www.blueletterbible.org/lang/lexicon/lexicon.cfm?t=kjv&strongs=g3997.
8. "Meek." *Merriam-Webster.* https://www.merriam-webster.com/dictionary/meek.
9. "Strong's G4239 – prays." *Blue Letter Bible.*

https://www.blueletterbible.org/lang/lexicon/
lexicon.cfm?Strongs=G4239&t=KJV.

10. Carson, D. A. *Scandalous*. Crossway, 2010, p. 31–32.

11. Sweeney, Nate. *Abiding in Identity*. Sermon To Book, 2018.

12. "Vance Havner Quote 7." *Sermon Index*. http://www.sermonindex.net/modules/myal-bum/photo.php?lid=3493.

13. Bianchi, Francesco. "Prince." In *Lexham Theological Wordbook*, edited by Douglas Mangum et al., Lexham Bible Reference Series (Lexham Press, 2014).

14. Louw, Johannes P., and Eugene Albert Nida. *Greek-English Lexicon of the New Testament: Based on Semantic Domains*. United Bible Societies, 1996, p. 144.

15. "Persecuted Church Statistics." *The Esther Project*. http://theestherproject.com/statistics.

16. "Global Restrictions on Religion Rise Moderately in 2015, Reversing Downward Trend." *Pew Research Center*. April 11, 2017. p. 5. http://www.pewfo-rum.org/2017/04/11/4-among-the-most-populous-countries-russia-egypt-india-pakistan-and-nigeria-had-highest-overall-restrictions-on-religion-in-2015.

17. Bonhoeffer, Dietrich. *The Cost of Discipleship*. Simon and Schuster, 1959.

18. Scalia, Antonin. In Craig Brian Larson and Brian Lowery, *1001 Quotations that Connect: Timeless Wisdom for Preaching, Teaching, and Writing*, Zondervan, 2009, p. 67.

19. Fleming, Rocky. "Journaling."

About the Author

Nate Sweeney would be considered an average person, someone who loves his family, community, and church. The major factor that sets him apart is his passion to Know Christ and Make Him Known. This vision is at the fore-front of Nate's daily focus and drives him to stay connected to Christ and share that relationship with oth-ers. Nate pursues this vision in his home with his wife, Monica, and their three kids.

Nate has served in many ministry capacities since he

graduated from Bible school in 1997. He is the directional leader of Catalyst Church in Bentonville, Arkansas. Nate is also the founder and directional leader of The Abiding Network, and he sits on the Influencers Ministry global board as a church relations leader.

Nate speaks with experience, as he has led his church to be transformed into an Abiding Church, and his role has become supported by the great leaders who have been raised up in this church. At the time of this publishing, Nate has mentored, coached, and helped disciple hundreds of church leaders nationally.

It is evident, through Nate's ministry, that people are challenged to daily experience God and grow in their relationship with Him, while discovering what He has called them to do in life and share His love in practical ways.

About Sermon To Book

SermonToBook.com began with a simple belief: that sermons should be touching lives, *not* collecting dust. That's why we turn sermons into high-quality books that are accessible to people all over the globe.

Turning your sermon series into a book exposes more people to God's Word, better equips you for counseling, accelerates future sermon prep, adds credibility to your ministry, and even helps make ends meet during tight times.

John 21:25 tells us that the world itself couldn't contain the books that would be written about the work of Jesus Christ. Our mission is to try anyway. Because in heaven, there will no longer be a need for sermons or books. Our time is now.

If God so leads you, we'd love to work with you on your sermon or sermon series.

Visit www.sermontobook.com to learn more.

Made in the USA
Columbia, SC
30 October 2018